Money
on't
Table

Money on't Table

GRIT, WORK AND FAMILY PRIDE

True Stories from the Boys and Girls of the
Manufacturing Heartlands of Britain

Corinne Sweet

1 3 5 7 9 10 8 6 4 2

First published in 2017 by September Publishing

Copyright © Corinne Sweet 2017

The right of Corinne Sweet to be identified as the author of this
work has been asserted by her in accordance with the Copyright
Designs and Patents Act 1988.

The photos on pages 9, 61, 121, 169 and 219 belong to the
contributors. Derek Happs and Pauline Braker's photos (pages
9 and 169) were both taken for Boots publicity campaigns.
The photo on page 263 is a magazine plate from 1954,
courtesy of The Advertising Archives.

Typeset by Ed Pickford

Printed in Denmark on paper from responsibly managed,
sustainable sources by Nørhaven

ISBN 978-1-910463-54-3

September Publishing
www.septemberpublishing.org

To the Potters, Haynes, Marshes, Ordishes and Rogers
who made me feel very at home in Nottingham

Particularly, for Corinne Haynes and in loving
memory of Albert Haynes

Contents

Preface

Nottingham: The Heartland of England

Nottinghamshire, 1930. A county in the Midlands right in the centre of England, bounded by Yorkshire, Lincolnshire, Leicestershire and Derbyshire. A rural county, yet with a heavily industrialised city at its heart. Nottingham was known for its tightly-packed, soot-encrusted, red-brick back-to-back terraced houses; smoke curling over cooling towers, barges on canals, trams and buses cutting through cobbled streets. Narrow lanes led to industrial yards and huge factories, and teemed with street sellers, and horses and drays led by cloth-capped workers. People made their way around town on foot or pushing sit-up-and-beg bicycles.

In the thirties, when this book begins, Nottingham was renowned for its manufacturing, and for three household names in particular: Boots the Chemist, Players cigarettes and Raleigh bicycles. There were other industries as well, names like Avery, Austin Reed and – in nearby Derby – Rolls-Royce. It was the heartland of England and chimed with national pride.

1

The Industrial Revolution transformed Nottingham from a graceful garden town in the 1750s to a place of dark satanic mills. Partly due to its geography, Nottingham became rapidly overpopulated and crowded. Built on a network of sandstone caves (locally it is known as the City of Caves), Nottingham had soggy meadows to the south and a sandstone crag to the west, upon which Nottingham Castle had been built after the Norman conquest. Established in 1796, the Nottingham Canal brought coal and other heavy goods to the city. In the 1820s alone, 3,000 back-to-back artisan dwellings were built. In a time of Empire and world export, Nottingham could produce and produce. However, it was often at the cost of the worker's health and welfare as working and living conditions were cramped and dangerous.

Industrialisation increased with the advent of steam. In 1829, George Stephenson's *Rocket* hailed the railways, and Netherfield, north of the city, became a railway frontier town. Steam engines were used in factories to speed up production, too, as mechanical looms replaced traditional hand weavers – who had worked at home around rural Nottinghamshire in this poorly paid domestic industry for two hundred years (William Lee, in Calverton, had invented framework knitting in 1589, and in 1750 there had been 1,200 frames), churning out lace, hosiery and textiles.

The rapid expansion of mid to late Victorian Nottingham gobbled up the surrounding countryside and villages, and turned them into factories with more badly housed workers. Slums were created in places that had once been rural idylls. In 1897, Nottingham became a city with nearly 250,000 inhabitants caught in an increasingly rigid class structure of owners and the owned.

And this is the Nottingham we remember (after Robin Hood and his band of Merry Men). We think of cricket at Trent Bridge, a gentleman's game enjoyed also by the working man. We think of whirring pit heads with black-faced miners, *Sons and Lovers* by D.H. Lawrence, lace and textile factories, boot and shoe makers, munitions works and blacksmiths, brick makers and steelworks. It is a hive of industry, a mass of shops and market stalls, with hardy workers toiling endlessly to earn a crust.

Nottingham remained a heavily industrialised city during the two world wars as it produced steel, iron and munitions. Women were commanded to take over men's jobs and then were returned to the hearth once the wars were over. Great poverty and hardship ensued for the women who were widowed or remained forever single.

Between the wars, the 1926 General Strike and the Great Depression of the 1930s hit Nottingham extremely hard. Two or three hundred starving men lined up for one job or walked miles to Leicester or Derby to try to get work. It was a desperate time for ordinary working people, who had no welfare service or reliable contraception to help keep their families healthy and small. Religion and pubs provided some comfort, although many people were Methodist teetotallers, who preached abstinence when it came to the demon drink.

Post-Second World War Nottingham was all about modernisation. Although the city had been bombed, many of the old factories and landmarks were still standing. From the 1950s onwards, there was a plan to sweep away the Victorian slums and replace them with high-rise buildings. Sadly, although people got indoor toilets and electric light, they lost the city's industrial heart when it was replaced by one-way systems, retail parks, concrete and glass, all in the name of progress. The destruction of whole areas of Nottingham, such as St Ann's and Radford, dismantled whole communities. Streets, churches, social centres and pubs were swept away and flattened. The landscape, culture and community were changed forever, tipped into new-build anonymity. Joan Wallace, a local writer, describes the traditional, vibrant, working-class Nottingham life in her book *Independent Street*, a depiction of her home in Radford pre-demolition. It's tough and rough, but there's a feeling of interconnectedness and community despite poverty and deprivation.

In 1958, Alan Sillitoe's *Saturday Night and Sunday Morning* shocked the country with its realistic portrayal of factory life. Based on the author's time working at 'the Raleigh', it depicted the hard-drinking, womanising, godless life that ensued from being a man chained to the production line. The book encapsulated industrial 'alienation'.

Nottingham is now a post-industrial city of the digital age. There are no mines left and only one 400-year-old lace framework factory: G.H. Hurt's in Chilwell, which recently supplied handcrafted shawls to Prince George and Princess Charlotte. The lace factories are gone, and museums (especially the Museum of Nottingham Life) are the only reminder of its glorious, fine-filigreed past.

Raleigh bikes were outridden in the marketplace by the Chinese, Taiwanese and Koreans, and the factory closed in 2002, moving production to the Far East. Players cigarettes also choked in 2014, laying off its last 544 workers in 2015 after the nation gave up nicotine or took to vaping. Boots the Chemist, still a high-street name, was bought by American giant Walgreens in 2014.

Nottingham's story epitomises that of industrial Britain in its shift from being a jewel in the Empire's crown to being a warehouse and importer of goods from elsewhere. Nottingham still has some light industry but, like the rest of the UK, it is focused more on service industries now. In a post-Brexit world, it would be hard-pressed to produce goods to export as it did in the nineteenth century.

However, there are still some amazing older people in Nottingham who can speak about their lives and times working in the now disappeared factories. This book is about their gritty stories and we follow a portion of their lives, from 1928 to about 1960. They have a lot in common: they all grew up in hardship, the nature of which we can hardly imagine today. The toilet was at the bottom of the yard, they had no running water, no central heating or even electricity in some cases, and certainly no TV, phone or other mod cons. It was a time of deprivation and hard work, but it was also an era of community, of sharing and caring, and learning to make do on very little.

In 1930, Boots had their main, purpose-built head-quarters in Beeston, Raleigh had a huge factory in Lenton and Players was in Radford. Each one had thousands of employees working in their main plants, warehouses and other outlets throughout Nottingham and beyond.

Labour was cheap and plentiful. The six men and women we'll meet were used to hearing about jobs on the social grapevine (street corners, local shops, the pub, at the work bench, family gossip), and many workers would leave a job one day and get another the next. The hunt was on constantly for that little bit of extra pay. For the six in this book, they knew they had to bring home money to add to the family coffers. There was no credit, they had to earn hard cash and save it, spending it mindfully and frugally. 'Make Do and Mend' was espoused by the government in the Second World War, but it was also the motto of these workers. There were no fancy foreign holidays – simply a day off in Skegness, a couple of days at Mablethorpe or a week at Great Yarmouth, if they were lucky.

All the events in this book are based on recollections of real-life events. Where necessary, I have recreated scenes and dialogue, but always with the aim of conveying the individual's life as truthfully as possible. I have changed names and other details to protect privacy and Bob Cox is a pseudonym.

The men and women in this book were resilient and faced life with good humour, despite experience of challenging events such as war, disease, disability, inequality, poverty and the death of loved ones. Hearing their fascinating stories is to be brought into direct contact with a way of life in the city now forever gone.

The Workers

Derek Happs (b. 1923) Now ninety-four, born in Hoyland Common, Barnsley, he moved to Nottingham once apprenticed to Boots.

Betty Allsop (b. 1926) Born and raised in the Meadows, Nottingham, and worked as a machinist (shirt maker). Betty is ninety years old.

Albert Godfrey (b. 1936) Albert worked in factories and became a gentleman's outfitter for Austin Reed. Now eighty, Albert was born and raised in Bulwell.

Pauline Braker (b. 1938) Born in Colwick, Betty worked at Boots, Players and other retail outlets, including becoming a corsetière. She is seventy-eight years old.

Doreen Rushton (b. 1944) Now seventy-two. Doreen was born in Netherfield, worked at Boots and fought her way to be a nurse.

Bob Cox (b. 1947) Bob was born in Radford and apprenticed to Raleigh, where he worked most of his life. He is now seventy.

Derek Happs

Derek mixing medicine at Boots pharmacy.

1

Trouble at t' Pit

On a cold, twilit evening in Hoyland Common, South Yorkshire in 1934, eleven-year-old Derek Happs peered anxiously down the cobbled street of stone-faced, back-to-back terraced houses. Two men were half-dragging, half-carrying a slumped figure with a bandaged head. Derek hovered by the peeling black front door, which led straight on to a short front garden path, while women in aprons and men in caps gathered on nearby doorsteps, arms crossed, silently watching the grim procession. Some raggedly dressed children ran to the three men as they lurched towards Derek's family home. A dog barked in the distance as Derek made out his father as one of the two men carrying the injured man, but he didn't recognise the other.

His mother Margaret stood patiently by the door with a white enamel bowl of water and a clean rag in her hands. 'Come away from the door, son. Yer'll only bother yer father.'

Obediently, Derek stepped back inside the dingy room and watched the proceedings through a small window.

His young sister Joan had crept into the room and was sitting at the bottom of the stairs, watching the scene with saucer eyes. Derek recognised the injured man from his square, muscular body and brown corduroy trousers. It was Dennis, his older half-brother, in a dazed, semi-conscious state. Ordinarily, Derek was wary of Dennis as he was usually threatening, shouting or using his fists to 'teach yer little booger a lesson', and his silence felt ominous. Yet, however free he was with his slaps, Dennis was his brother and Derek didn't want anything to happen to him.

He heard his father's voice on the doorstep. 'Ayup, easy, lad. That's it, bring 'im in 'ere.'

Derek retreated back further into the unlit kitchen-cum-living-room, and stood by the butler sink and wooden drainer under the window. Dennis was deposited heavily onto the cold stone floor. Margaret knelt by her son's body and carefully unwrapped the bandages, reveal-ing a huge horseshoe of blood on the back of his head, which oozed constantly. Derek shivered at the sight; not only at the blood, but also at seeing the usually vital Dennis so prone. How serious was it? Derek felt fear grip his intestines.

'Reckon 'e'll need a stitch,' Margaret whispered as she wiped the blood away, 'but it'll cost.'

Tiptoeing from the sink to just behind his mother, Derek watched the proceedings. 'We can tek it from 'ere,

Josh,' Thomas, Derek's father, said to the other man. 'You tek care of y'sel' now, lad.'

Now, in the half-light of the room, Derek could see that Josh was not much older than him, probably just twelve or thirteen, but his workman's clothes, belt, braces and boots, and his filthy face and rough hands, marked him out as a working man from the pit. Derek became self-conscious of his primary school uniform, with its navy pullover and grey shorts. Josh looked Derek up and down with a superior air, then doffed his worsted cap to Derek's mother – 'Mrs 'Apps' – before swaggering out the door like a proper grown up, making Derek feel very uncomfortable indeed. Derek was bookish and shy, and had a stutter, and was used to the local lads ribbing him, but he felt small and useless in comparison to Josh.

A groan from the body on the floor brought Derek back to the scene. Thomas, standing hands on hips and covered in grime, stared at Dennis, as if mesmerised by his battered state. 'It were a rock fall, a real bad 'un. Right after dinnertime.' Thomas's voice was hoarse with suppressed emotion. He wiped his face with the back of his hand, smearing coal dust and sweat over his face. 'We hadn't got a chance. Some died, many were injured … it were chaos, utter mayhem … it's the third fall this year …'

'He'll need a stitch,' Margaret said softly again, still wiping the wound with care. The white bowl on the stone floor was now dark with blood. 'We'll need to fetch the doctor.'

Derek didn't know what he should do, but the kitchen was becoming ever more gloomy as darkness fell, so he went to the black iron range in the alcove and lit a taper from the oven, ignited the wick of a paraffin lamp, then held it above his mother as she ripped up one of his father's old pit shirts to make into a fresh bandage. The lamp cast a ghoulish glow over the proceedings, and Derek watched in helpless fascination as his parents tended to their injured son. What if Dennis died? What if he was damaged permanently or needed constant care? He feared his brother, but he feared life even more without his wages, which had become essential to the household.

The doctor was only fetched in the direst of circumstances, but this was clearly a serious emergency. 'The Doctor Man' came round on a Friday, collecting money as a kind of medical insurance. Derek's mother paid into it, as did most of their neighbours, as doctors were expensive. Lots of people in the village resorted to traditional remedies made from herbs to treat illness and wounds. Dennis's injuries, however, seemed more serious than what old wives' tales and natural remedies could fix. Derek looked from parent to parent, keeping quiet while they worked out what to do. They always sorted things out between them, in a calm and equitable way.

Dennis moaned again, and his eyelids flickered.

Thomas dropped heavily to his knees and put his hands together. 'Oh, Lord Jesus, hear my prayer.' He sounded desperate and exhausted. 'Please save our Dennis, and bless the poor souls of the others who were taken from us, this dark day.'

Thomas's voice cracked, and he looked up at Derek, gesturing that he, too, should kneel in prayer.

Joan had crept over to join the family and was standing behind her mother's skirts, peeking out at Dennis. Derek put the lamp on a rickety chest of drawers, and knelt beside his father. His mother and Joan joined them, and all four clasped their hands and closed their eyes, over Dennis's groaning, prone body.

'Oh Lord, please guide the pit bosses to mek us safe, and heed our demands. Please save my dear brothers, and my dear son, who were crushed this very day …'

Derek opened an eye only to see his father had a tear running down his soot-encrusted face, so he pressed his hands together as hard as he could, and screwed up his eyes, knowing his father meant every single word with all his heart.

Although life went on the same in the days and weeks after the pit fall, the course of Derek's life was set to change. Dennis was off work for two weeks, having seen the doctor, and had twenty stitches. Luckily, he healed rapidly, so started work again, as he was not the kind of man to lie about at home, especially as the family needed the money. Eventually, the only reminder of the incident was a horse-shoe shape on the back of Dennis's head, where his hair never grew back properly. Meanwhile, the daily 'Knocker Upper' still came round as early as 5am, and rapped on the door to get Thomas and Dennis up for their shifts.

At the time, there was no welfare state, no compensation for injury or allowances made for disabilities caused on the job. It was expected that miners lived a rough and tough life and took what came in their hardy stride. The 1926 General Strike, followed by the Wall Street Crash in 1929, had led to the Great Depression and over two million unemployed in Britain. By 1934 there was a National Government made up of all three parties, headed up by Ramsay MacDonald, the ex-Labour prime minister. Derek would listen to his father preach about 'The State of the Working Man', and the importance of community, sacrifice, love and tolerance, especially in times of hardship. At his darkest point, Thomas had applied to emigrate to Australia but, despite getting a paid passage for his family, decided not to go as he felt a loyalty to his community and to his calling.

Thomas had been a miner for nearly thirty years. Miners like him were the backbone of the economy and kept the nation ticking over with their hard-hewn coal, so there was pride in the work, despite it being incredibly dangerous. The pit never closed, as coal was produced twenty-four hours a day, and the wheels of the pit shaft never stopped turning. Thomas and Dennis worked a range of shifts: either from six in the morning to two in the afternoon, or from two in the afternoon to ten at night, or worst of all an 'all nighter', from ten at night until six in the morning. Often, Derek and Joan would be going to school just as their father or Dennis slumped back in, exhausted; or they'd be going to bed as their father or Dennis went out briskly into the night.

The men took a quart bottle full of water with them (other men took beer, but the teetotal Methodists refrained), plus a 'snap' of bread and lard sandwiches; the snap got its name from the tin box the men used with a distinctive snap fastening. Margaret's job was to stay at home, to do the housework; the washing, the shopping and mending – all with no mod cons – and to tend to her family as they came and went to work or school.

One Friday night, soon after Dennis was back at work, Thomas was in the kitchen, putting on his one and only double-breasted navy blue serge suit. He had showered at the pit, which offered a communal hot wash for the men, and had donned a white, Robin-starched collar, fixed by a stud at the back of his best white shirt. It was all finished off with a sober black tie. While his father gave his boots a shine with Cherry Blossom, Derek was at the kitchen sink, he had propped up his book on the wooden drainer and was reading by the light of the window.

'Ahm going t'reckon, son,' said Thomas, 'will't come? You can play t'organ fer me, if you like.'

Derek knew this was a weekly ritual at the pit head, where the miners' gang leader shared out the week's wages to the men standing or squatting in a semi-circle. Afterwards, most of the men headed for the Hare and Hounds, the Keys or the Star to quench their hard-earned thirst, but Derek's father, now in his best suit, would be off to lay preach in local chapels. Thomas took real pride in looking scrubbed and respectable for his lay-preaching appointments.

Derek closed his book, washed his face and hands at the tap, and slicked his hair down with some water and a comb. From the age of nine Derek had been learning to play the organ with his uncle Cyril, Thomas's brother, who lived nearby, and found he had a real feeling for music. He loved playing hymns and popular songs, and now played regularly at chapel, even though he was still a young lad. He would get a few pennies or even a shilling or two, which would go into the family's coffers, so he felt he was doing his bit. He also loved hearing his father preach, as his heartfelt words and prayers, and people's reactions to what his father said, always filled him with pride. However, just before they left home, there was a rap at the front door, and Derek opened it.

'Evening Mr Styan,' said Derek politely to the squat, dark-haired man on the doorstep.

'Ayup, lad. It's time we had my tape measure round you again. My, you've grown.'

Derek looked down, self-consciously, at his grey school shorts – which had already been let down twice – hovering way above his knobbly knees, and just smiled weakly at Mr Styan, not sure of what to say. Meanwhile, Margaret was delving into the Lyons tea tin in the kitchen cupboard, and came forward proffering the weekly sum for the local tailor. ''Ere yer 're, Mr Styan.' This was the only way the family could save towards a new preaching suit for Thomas, a shilling or a few pennies at a time.

Then father and son set off through the cobbled village streets at dusk and passed a local man on a bicycle lighting the street gas lamps with his long pole with a hook at the end. 'Evening, Maurice,' said Derek's father.

'Evening, Thomas.'

There were no cars, and only a few bicycles. Some locals still had ponies and traps or carts, but most people still went by 'Shanks's pony' – on foot. After visiting the pit head, the pair strode on in silence towards Chapel Street. Thomas said, 'Yer a bright lad, son, and yer good at yer books. D'yer think yer can pass?'

Derek knew his father was referring to the eleven-plus exam, which the headmaster of Hoyland Primary, Mr Brodie, had suggested he sit. There had been a long discussion about Derek trying for the prestigious local grammar school, but his parents had finally, and sadly, concluded it was just too expensive in terms of bus travel, school uniform, sports equipment, trips and so on. Derek thought hard for a moment: he loved reading, he loved history as he wanted to know about ancient civilisations and languages, and he loved facts, especially medical and scientific ones. He'd absorbed as much information as he could, poring over the school's *Pears' Cyclopaedia*.

'I d–d–do, F–F–Father,' said Derek, thoughtfully.

'Well, yer mother and I have thought again, lad, and we think yer should have a go fer't grammar.'

Derek's eyes widened and he looked sideways at his father, who was striding ahead briskly in his smart suit and tie, with his best worsted cap pulled low at a jaunty angle over his forehead and steel-rimmed glasses.

'B–b–b–but—' started Derek.

'No buts, lad. The Lord will find a way. Ah don't want yer down the pit, like me and our Dennis. Yer can do better, I know yer can.' They reached the plain door of the Wesleyan Methodist Chapel with its windows glowing invitingly in the semi-darkness. 'After the pit fall I thought about it afresh, son. Ah don't want yer to work there, with the dust and gases, lung diseases, let alone the rock falls … If yer work hard, son, ah know yer can mek something of yersel'.'

Derek felt a lump come to his throat, a mixture of fear

and excitement. He had harboured a secret passion to try for the grammar along with another boy, Simon Arkin, in the village, who was also top of the class. Simon was set to go, as his parents could just afford it, but Derek had ruled it out. The cost had seemed an impossible barrier to Derek, and he remembered his parents talking at length in the yard about it. 'B–b–but the c–c–cost …' said Derek, looking at his father's calm face.

'We'll find a way,' said Thomas, straightening his tie and smoothing his hair. 'The Lord will provide. Yer just focus on yer books, lad. Now, let's get on. We've a job to do 'ere, the Lord's work. 'Appen that's quite important, eh, lad?'

2

Hard-Earned Place

After his talk with his father, Derek resolved to be extra helpful at home as a thank you to his hard-pressed parents, and to focus as much as possible on his exams.

His mother and father were unusually old for parents at the time, in their forties when he had been born in 1923. Both had lost their first spouses to fatal illness, which is how Thomas had another son, Dennis. He also had a daughter, Joyce, who was now married and living away. Sadly, Thomas's first wife Bertha had died of consumption – tuberculosis – which was rife, especially among the poor. A couple of years later, Thomas met Margaret, who was working as a housekeeper for a local doctor, at chapel. She was widowed, as Langford, her first husband, had died, as had her two small daughters, of chest infections. Infant and childhood illnesses were common and often fatal at that time, due to the lack of antibiotics and general poor health and nutrition. So Derek and his younger sister Joan were the progeny of the happy mid-life relationship between Thomas and Margaret, who were deeply in love and well suited, despite their ages and poverty.

Their two-up, two-down house had a trench or a 'midden' out the back, which was a communal lavatory, with cut-up newspaper on a string for toilet paper. The midden was emptied once a week by a local man, but it smelled, and often flooded when it rained, and Derek hated it, craving privacy. He would whistle or sing to make sure people knew he was hidden behind the wooden panels. The only way up to the terrace's two bedrooms was by a staircase in the backyard, a freezing journey in the raw elements. The family – Joan and parents in one room, and Dennis and Derek in the other – had chamber pots for night use, and these would be tipped into the midden in the morning.

As there was no bathroom, the whole family shared a weekly tin bath, which was brought in from the back-yard where it hung by handles from a hook on the wall. Water was heated on the stove and then carbolic soap and a flannel, or even a bristle brush, was used on black necks, knees, hands and feet. The water was topped up as it cooled, but it got scummier and murkier as the baths continued – woe betide who got the last bath. The coal-heated range had a box built in to heat water, and it was Derek and Joan's job to go and scavenge for sticks and bits of coal to keep it going. As cooking was done on it, and tea 'mashed' (made) regularly, it was a pretty important job.

Shortly after Thomas told Derek he could try for grammar school, Derek was with his mother and sister in the living room. 'Is there owt ah can do fer yer?' he asked his mother.

'Have yer done yer extra study?' she asked, not looking up from the sink where she was washing dishes.

'Yes, Mother. Can ah do owt else?'

Margaret thought for a moment, and then said, 'Yer can tek the battery for charging, it's low.'

Derek knew exactly what she meant, as their relatively new Ecko Bakelite-cased wireless had a heavy rectangular battery which he would take to the local garage in a shoebox where it was charged overnight for a few pennies. Once charged, the battery was good for about twenty hours' worth of radio time. Derek remembered the whole family gathering round the Ecko and listening to King George V make the first ever Christmas broadcast on it in December 1932. It had seemed magical to hear the King's voice floating across the kitchen-cum-living-room on the airwaves, something he never forgot.

Another day his mother asked, 'If yer've nowt to do, could you tek a brush and whitewash upstairs, lad?'

Derek had learned the rudiments of whitewashing and paper hanging from his mother, and enjoyed helping out with house repairs, which always seemed numerous, particularly as his father and brother worked such long, strange hours and were always short of sleep.

Other family jobs Derek took on were more arduous, such as cobbling the family's shoes. They couldn't afford to go to a proper cobbler, so Thomas had fashioned a 'last' and Derek was sent to the church warden, who had leather offcuts he could buy. Then Thomas taught Derek how to mend soles by putting the shoes on the last, stretching the leather and using a strong glue to keep it in place. It was a dirty, smelly job, which Derek found tough to do, but he felt he was contributing to the household.

The whole family would have a go at making rag rugs, which were made by cutting up old clothes into short strips, and then 'pegging' – poking them through a piece of canvas stretched on a wooden frame with a special metal tool (made by Thomas). The rugs were needed to cover the bare, cold floors, and wore out with all the boots flattening and battering them daily. Derek took charge of pegging. He helped his mother beat the rugs, but he also wanted to relieve his mother of making them, too, as she was always busy washing, ironing, knitting, cleaning, cooking and sewing for everyone.

Since the age of seven, Derek had also done odd jobs in the village for money, such as collecting weekly subs house to house for Mrs Scarrot who ran a Christmas Club draw for the local grocery shop. When the rag-and-bone man came by on his horse and cart, ringing a hand bell and shouting his usual guttural 'Raggabun' cry to take away any unwanted goods, Derek would fetch and carry for him for a few pennies. He loved getting a balloon or even a goldfish in a jam jar in return for scavenging an old brass bedstead or piece of metal, discarded in an alleyway.

Catering for a family of five on meagre wages was tough, so Derek helped his mother as much as he could. 'Can yer come to the market wi' me, lad?' Margaret would say, as she handed him two baskets to carry, on a Friday afternoon. She would buy family provisions with the end-of-week wages, from black sewing thread to a small joint of pork for the Sunday dinner, the remnants of which would be stretched out for several days.

Thomas, and sometimes Dennis, grew vegetables and fruit on the community allotment, but they were seasonal and didn't last long. In autumn, Margaret spent hours making jam and chutneys and the children were set to topping and tailing gooseberries and blackberries, or coring and chopping apples and onions, and sterilising a battery of Kilner jam jars. Derek's uncle Cyril killed a pig in the autumn, which Derek helped him salt, burn off bristles and preserve. His reward would be a pig's head or trotters or a hock to take home and boil.

Margaret stretched every penny, and taught Derek to be thrifty and to bargain gracefully over purchases.

Derek also collected milk for the family, in a white enamel churn, from a local farm, which was warm to hug as he stomped home along the lane bringing it back for breakfast. However, the lovely, creamy milk had to be watered down to keep it going for a few days. Then the 'balm man' would come to the door twice a week selling blocks of yeast in two huge wicker baskets, and Margaret would buy a chunk. 'D'yer want to gi' me a hand kneading, children?' she'd ask, and indeed, Derek and Joan were taught to knead bread between each proving stage on the black cast-iron range.

Bread was the mainstay of every meal, and Margaret would make a loaf most days: there was often very little else to eat but bread. Margaret would say to Derek and Joan, 'Come and stand to the table, children,' and they would be given a chunk of bread, a glass of water, and a dot of either dripping or tomato ketchup, which they spread around their plates skilfully with the bread. They stood to the table as there were no chairs. Sometimes after school, Derek and Joan went to the local working men's club to get a daily free hand-out of bread and dripping, as it helped to keep them from hunger when the Happs' family rations were running low.

'Open it, son.' Thomas watched as Derek held the heavy cream envelope in his hand, weighing its contents.

'Come on, courage, lad,' piped up Margaret.

27

Derek went out into the backyard and held his breath for a moment as he ripped open the letter: it was just a short, officious paragraph, addressed to 'Mr Thomas Happs', but his father allowed Derek to open it himself. Derek's heart pumped wildly as he read, 'We are delighted to be able to offer your son, Derek Happs, a place ...'

Grinning wildly, Derek ran back inside to where his parents were waiting. Thomas read the letter carefully, and looked back up at Derek, beaming, pointing at a paragraph with his finger, 'Yer see 'ere, son, did yer see this?'

Derek looked over his father's shoulder, almost afraid, and then read the word 'scholarship'. His parents wrapped their arms round him.

'Well done, son,' said Margaret, tears in her eyes.

'It's a miracle, son,' said Thomas, warmly, clapping him on the back. 'What did I tell yer? The Lord has provided. He has answered all our prayers.'

3

'A Gentlemanly Youth Wanted'

'Ahm sorry, son, ah really am, but it's just not possible.' Thomas Happs was holding a piece of paper that Derek had just handed to him.

It was a sunny summer's afternoon in June 1938, and Derek was now fifteen. Going to Ecclesfield Grammar School had opened the world to him. From wonderful books and ideas, Latin and Greek, poetry and scientific knowledge, to the complexities of cricket scoring and rugby, and to the possibility of a wider life.

Mr Helmsley, the headmaster, had called Derek into his office after the matriculation exams were finished. 'You show exceptional promise,' he had said to the self-effacing, gangly young man before him. 'Have you considered university?'

Derek's eyes widened. 'University?'

He knew his grammar school friend Benji was going to go there, as his family had come into some money from a distant relative. He looked shyly at Mr Helmsley, behind his hefty oak desk piled with papers, and then at the Persian carpet, 'N—no, s—sir,' was all he could get out.

'Well, I think you should,' Mr Helmsley said. 'There are ways and means, you know, scholarships, bursaries … You could do languages, or sciences, you have talent.'

Derek was flabbergasted. 'Ah'll talk to my father,' was all Derek could say.

All the way home on the bus Derek imagined himself sitting in a lofty library, rather like the school one, with Gothic architecture and beautiful leather-lined books neatly stacked alphabetically on wall-to-ceiling shelves. He loved learning, reading and finding things out; he also loved writing neatly with pen and ink, and constructing paragraphs about the English Revolution and Cromwell, or analysing Charles Reade's *The Cloister and the Hearth* or John Milton's *Paradise Lost*. He still played the organ in church on Sundays, and had sung at school in the choir, learning more about the rudiments of musical theory.

However, Derek knew, even as he handed his father the letter on heavy paper from Mr Helmsley, which suggested that Derek apply to university, that it was a lost cause. It was not that his father wanted to hold him back, or begrudge him a better life than his – far from it – it just all came down to something very simple: economics. They were too poor to consider Derek going away for three years and not contributing to the household.

This was complicated by the fact that a year earlier Derek's mother had begun to get seriously ill. She had endured rheumatoid arthritis as a child, and then as a married woman had exhausted herself nursing her first husband and two children until they died. All this happened before she was thirty. After that she had been in service working long hours, and now, in her second marriage, with two more children and a stepson to care for, and living in such gruelling poverty, she suffered a fair amount of physical hardship. Margaret's life had not been one of ease, and she had bouts when she simply had to retreat to bed.

Derek had even been sent away a couple of times to live with Aunty Annie and Uncle Horace, who kept pigs and had quite a bit more money than the Happs. But now Margaret was increasingly unwell, and unable to work at all. Dennis had left the household to get married and while Thomas was bringing in a miner's wage it barely covered their day-to-day expenses, and Joan couldn't help much as she was still at school. Although Derek had a scholarship, there were some school expenses that the family still had to meet that were difficult for them to afford.

Thomas had also been talking to Derek about the ominous gathering storm in Europe and what it might mean for them all. There was talk of war again, something that Thomas dreaded after the last one in which he served in the trenches. There was plenty of news in the papers and on the wireless about a Mr Adolf Hitler in Germany who was stirring things up, and, in September 1938, Prime Minister Neville Chamberlain would make an agreement with him (useless, as it soon famously turned out to be) to keep the peace. There was unease and uncertainty in the air at home, too, following the Depression when so many working people, including their family, had nearly starved to death; in fact, some actually had. The spectre of poverty was never far from Thomas's mind's eye, and he wanted better for his son.

'Ah wish it were different, son,' Thomas continued, passionately. 'Ahm so sorry, but we need you to work, to go and get a job.'

Derek wasn't bitter, or angry, as he respected his father hugely. He was worried about his mother's ailing health, and sorely wanted to help. He knew he had had a wonderful chance to go to the grammar, and his parents had enabled him to take it, with quite a lot of sacrifice. The family had never had a holiday, only the very occasional picnic or half-day out. Their only regular social activities were Methodist Church events or formal family gatherings, such as christenings, weddings and funerals. Despite his family's abject poverty, Derek had been brought up with sincerity, love and care, and he accepted his fate sadly but with equanimity. He knew, even then, that his exposure to learning and ideas had changed him and given him something to work towards. He would always have his love of history, novels and poetry, and of facts, figures and learning, to carry him through tough times.

Thomas could see that his son would strive to do well, wherever he was placed. 'Ah will not let yer go down the pit,' Thomas said. 'Ah promised that years ago. We will find you a better position than that.'

The card in the window of the shop said, 'We have a vacancy for a gentlemanly youth to train in the pharmacy.'

Thomas and Derek were standing outside a Boots the Chemist shop in Barnsley. Derek was fascinated by the two huge curved glass bottles with giant stoppers standing in the window, one filled with purple watery liquid and the other with green. Both Thomas and Derek were dressed up in their Sunday best, although Derek was sporting a black eye and a limp from a rather energetic game of football on the previous Saturday.

'See son,' said Thomas, encouragingly, 'they want grammar school boys, like you. Gentlemanly men.'

Derek smiled at his father, who was always so thoughtful and kind towards him. Thomas always tried to see the positive side, so Derek resolved, there and then, that he would, too. He held his breath to gain courage, as they entered the wooden shelf-lined shop, which was a marvellous emporium with every kind of remedy, potion and lotion on view.

Once inside the tiny office of Mr Gough, the

manager,' Thomas and Derek perched on two high-backed chairs beside the roll-top desk. Mr Gough was an orderly man in a brown pinstriped suit with a waist-coat. His hair was trimmed close to his head and gold spectacles perched on the end of his nose. He read Derek's letter of application, written in a neat long-hand. 'I see you've done very well at the grammar,' said Mr Gough, peering over his glasses at Derek, who blushed. 'Very good results, boy.'

Derek picked a piece of fluff carefully off his rather too-short shorts, which were revealing livid weals and multicoloured bruises on his legs and knees.

Mr Gough cleared his throat. 'Young man, I am pleased to discuss the offer of a position in the pharmacy here that would not just be a job, but ...' he paused significantly, 'if, and I mean if, the candidate did well it might actually lead to an apprenticeship with Boots the Chemist.'

He went on to say that Boots was an extremely respectable, well-established company, going back to John and Mary Boot's first remedy shop in Goose Gate in Nottingham in 1849, when it was called the Boot Pure Drug Company. Jesse Boot, their son, had taken over the business on his father's early demise, and Boots now had over a thousand stores, with The Booklovers' Library in 450 of them, and even tearooms in some of the bigger ones. 'Anyone worth their salt would be proud of the opportunity to work for Boots,' he said with an emphatic sniff.

His spiel over, Mr Gough turned to Derek, and looked at him pointedly over his gold rims, 'So, tell me, young Derek, what qualities am I looking for?'

This was far worse than Derek had expected and he had no idea what to say. He could feel Mr Gough's gaze piercing into his forehead as he stared at the knots in the wooden floorboards. He had to say something sensible, so he tried to begin, 'Ah, ah, ah, ahm willing to learn, s–sir.'

Mr Gough was not very impressed. He looked back at the paper, showing Derek's outstanding results, and then at Derek, with his long bruised legs, shy demeanour and stutter. 'I see,' he said, not sure that he did. How could he possibly consider training up such a shy being, despite him being so good on paper? How could the boy deal with the public?

Seeing the difficulty of the situation, Thomas, who was naturally charismatic and a good speaker, spoke up for his son. 'Mr Gough,' he began, 'my son, well, he might be a bit shy, but he has qualities of honesty and integrity. He's played the organ in Hoyland Church since he was twelve, he was largely self-taught, and has worked very hard at the grammar and got good results. They want him to stay on, to go to the university, but he needs to work.' Thomas looked Mr Gough straight in the eye as he said, for emphasis, 'Ah don't want him down the pit, like mesel', it's far too dangerous. He's a sensitive lad, a bright lad, he's got a good head on his shoulders and ah believe he'll go far. He's a hard worker and ah think you should give him a chance.'

Derek spent the whole of this speech blushing to his roots, which highlighted the gingery gold of his hair. He still stared at the wooden floor, but took an occasional peek at Mr Gough who was looking thoughtfully between Thomas and Derek.

'Hmmm, I see,' he said. Mr Gough then took another long look at Derek, who had recovered his composure a bit, and was now returning his gaze.

Derek felt overwhelmed by his father's praise and very moved by his words. He wanted to make his father proud, so he sat up straight and smiled as warmly as he could at Mr Gough.

Deciding, the manager turned back to his desk, dipped his pen in his ink pot and started writing a letter on the crisp white headed paper.

As they all stood up to leave he held out his hand for Thomas to shake, then shook Derek's and said, 'All right, Derek will start here in two weeks. I've recommended him to head office in Nottingham. Let's see what he can do.'

4

Learning on the Job

On his first day at work in the Boots pharmacy, Mr Gough sat Derek down and gave him a sign that said: 'The customer is always right.'

'This, Derek, was Jesse Boot's saying and it's the motto we work by here,' said Mr Gough. 'You have to learn to pay attention to what the customer wants and then find a way of satisfying their needs. We never like them to go away empty-handed, if at all possible.'

Derek took a mental note. He had told Mr Gough in his interview that he was willing to learn, and he meant it. Then Mr Gough showed him the prescription book, a huge ledger in which he had to write, in pen and ink at the top, the date and day in Latin. Then all the drugs given out were listed, in Latin, in pen and ink by the pharmacist, so a proper record of dispensations was kept.

At first, Derek was overawed by the number of products, remedies and items, and by all their myriad names.

Mr Gough handed Derek a huge, red leather-covered tome called *British Pharmacopoeia*, which had pages and pages of Latin names of drugs and preparations. 'This is what you would have to learn if you trained,' explained Mr Gough. 'It can take years.'

It became clear to Derek that he was, at first, to learn the trade simply by selling bars of Pears' soap, Collis Browne's cough mixture or nit combs, and by observing Mr Gough, who was not only the manager but a qualified pharmacist. The shop had wooden counters, with glass tops and divisions underneath, where a lot of the medicines were stored in little brown glass bottles or white packets.

'Now Derek,' said Mr Gough in a serious tone, 'you are not to recommend anything to a customer at this point, do you understand? You always have to refer to myself or a senior member of staff.'

'Y–yes, of course, M–Mr G–Gough.'

Derek was given a yellow cloth and told to dust along the chemist counter and shelves, cleaning all the items and reading their names: 'Acriflavine', 'Proflavine', 'Chloramine-T'. Derek spent hours poring over the bottles and boxes, taking in their names and looking them up, and began to learn what they did or didn't do.

He was a conscientious worker, and very soon Mr Gough recommended him to be offered a proper apprenticeship. Derek was thrilled, as were his parents, so he signed on the dotted line, with his proud father present as a witness – 'Well done, son' – with the knowledge that he would soon be taken through the *British Pharmacopoeia* in fine and extensive detail, so he could really understand his job.

After about six months he was beginning to feel more relaxed and happy, and he noticed that even his stutter was receding as he gained confidence and experience. Mr Gough was particularly pleased. One day, the bell on the door trilled and Derek turned to find his mother standing there, beaming, in her Sunday best and clutching her handbag. He was thrilled and blushed. He had no idea how she had afforded the bus fare to visit him, but knew intuitively she wanted to see him 'at work' as a surprise.

Derek pulled himself up straight, smoothed his white coat and said, 'Can I help you, madam?' with sincere earnestness. Then they both broke into smiles and Derek's mother leaned over the counter and patted his sleeve with maternal pride, for reply. Derek felt tears prick his eyes.

Apart from his mother's surprise visit, which knocked him sideways, he was also learning how to deal with the wider public, which wasn't always easy. On one occasion, an attractive young woman entered the shop in a blue hat and matching coat.

'Excuse me,' she said to Derek, who stood behind the counter in a white coat, 'I want something to get rid of a corn.'

By now, Derek had begun to learn something useful about the simpler remedies for everyday problems such as mouth ulcers, sunburn, head lice and corns. He picked up a packet: 'Th–th–this is Boots corn and wart solvent, it contains salicylate acid, and it will kill the corn. There is also Indian hemp in it, and that will kill the pain.' He watched the information register with the young woman. 'Ah–ah–ah recommend you put Vaseline round the corn and apply this in the evening, with the little brush supplied, before bed every night. The Vaseline will stop the solution getting on your skin.'

'Oh, I see,' said the young lady, taking the box and looking at it intently.

'It will kill your corn in a week.' Derek was pleased with his effort. 'It's sixpence,' he finished.

The young lady was just opening her handbag to purchase the treatment when a small woman in a black coat shuffled up to her, curlers showing under her black knitted hat. She'd been watching the proceedings at the counter from near the door.

'Don't take any notice of him,' she said to the woman in blue, to Derek's amazement. 'My grandmother says the way t' get rid of a corn is to go to't butcher's shop, get a tiny bit of meat, then tek it home, tek some black cotton, tie it to the bough of a tree and spin it round, clockwise. The next day tek it an' rub yer corn anticlockwise with the bit of meat and yer corn will go in two or three minutes. My grandmother says there's nowt better.'

'Oh?' said the young lady in surprise.

'It won't cost you owt, either,' said the woman in curlers, with a satisfied sniff.

Derek watched this exchange with open fascination and some consternation, especially when the young woman turned back to him and said, 'I'm not bothered today, thank you,' and promptly left the shop.

An hour later she returned, and Derek smiled at her, thinking that she had had second thoughts and that he had finally made the sale. However, the woman in blue simply asked, 'Can you tell me where I can find the nearest butcher's shop?'

Derek was flabbergasted, but directed her to Underwoods. With a wry smile, he could almost hear Mr Gough saying the Boots maxim: 'The customer is always right.'

Broken-Hearted

Derek's apprenticeship lasted four years, from the age of sixteen to twenty. However, during this time two hugely momentous things occured: tragically, his mother died in his first year of work; then Britain went to war with Germany and her allies.

It had been a terrible thing for Derek to see his mother decline, getting weaker and weaker and needing to stay in bed more frequently and for longer periods. Although his family never talked openly about her illness, Derek knew her condition was something to do with a weak heart due to the rheumatic arthritis she suffered from as a child.

When it was apparent she was nearing the end, Derek stayed home with her for a couple of days as he couldn't bear for her to be alone. His heartbroken father continued to go to work – he had to, for the money – but Derek sat beside his mother, held her hand, read poetry to her, and sang gentle songs and hymns, while he fed her teaspoons of brandy to ease her pain. At the very end he cradled her in his arms, tears running down his cheeks.

Her death left Derek utterly distraught. He was only

sixteen, and he loved his mother dearly. How could she be gone? His mother was his champion, his backbone, his sincere and stalwart carer.

Thomas came home and cried with him, and prayed over his dear wife's dead body. Derek left him alone, but could hear his father's grieving throughout the house. Joan held on to Derek and sobbed her little heart out: their happy family was no more. The only saving grace was, in Derek's mind, that their family had indeed been happy. For that, he thanked the Lord. Just like his father had taught him to do.

For a while after the simple funeral, Derek developed a nervous habit of flicking his hair back by jerking his head to the side, due to suppressed grief and anxiety. By then Derek was working in a new Boots shop in Rotherham with a Mr Cronk.

One day Mr Cronk took Derek into his office to talk to him about something important. Mr Cronk cleared his throat and said, quite gently, 'Ah've noticed yer coming to work with dirty collars, Derek.'

Uncharacteristically, Derek burst into tears and couldn't stop. He sobbed his heart out. Mr Cronk moved a chair under him and Derek sat heavily, put his head in his hands and cried very hard. Mr Cronk closed the door and left him in peace. Life with his father and little sister was chaotic without his mother around to run the household.

Mr Cronk came back in and said to Derek, after he'd blown his nose hard, 'When yer've finished yer duty of work today, I want you to get a bus and come to our house and stay wi' us for a while, son.'

He handed Derek a piece of paper with his address on it. Derek still could hardly speak, so he just nodded, his face mottled and flushed.

That evening, he posted a note to his father, explaining the situation, and then got the bus to Mr Cronk's house and had a proper wash and a good meal. Mrs Cronk served a high tea of pork chops, potatoes and cabbage, and Derek ate it gratefully. Even though they had to spend a few hours in the Anderson shelter during a bombing raid that night, Derek felt more refreshed in the morning. He'd got some sleep, albeit in a dank bunk, until the 'all clear' sounded. Then he'd had breakfast in the morning with Mr Cronk's three chatty daughters, who were still at school. They cheered him up and made him smile.

Derek stayed for a few weeks, and Mrs Cronk washed and starched his collars, mended the holes in his socks and helped him start to feel himself again. All this help was offered to Derek without a word about rent or paying his way, it was simply understood that he was in dire straits, mourning his mother at just sixteen years of age, and understandably not dealing with it all very well. Mr Cronk was there in Derek's hour of need and Derek never forgot it.

Derek's poor bereaved father continued to work down the mine, as coal was needed badly to keep the home fires burning during the war. He kept home for Joan and Derek, as the latter came and went to different placements with Boots. Thomas was too old to sign up with the military, and had injuries from the previous conflict which prevented him from being on active service.

Bombing raids happened regularly, some of the worst in 1941. Derek was a firewatcher, which meant looking out for incendiaries setting fires in the village. The surrounding area was constantly being blitzed – cities and towns such as Sheffield, Derby, Rotherham, Barnsley, Coventry and Nottingham were all under attack, as the Germans targeted and pounded the industrial centres, trying to destroy British might and resolve. However, canny farmers outside of the cities set decoy fires in fields to try and make the bombers drop their lethal loads onto green grass instead of valuable factories, and as a ploy it often worked quite well.

Boots offered Derek a fairly generous deal to retain his services during the war. He told his boss he wanted to join the army, but Boots's management had spotted his talents and wanted to keep him for as long as they could. He continued as an apprentice for his four-year stint, but was also attached to an army training centre on a scheme with the Royal Engineers. Boots asked him to return to their employment after the war, and he signed a document committing to that, so they paid him a retainer while he was training up with the army: it was called articles of pupillage. Thus, while Derek was working at Boots, he was also sent off to Wakefield to train in civil and mechanical engineering for the army, coming away with a diploma. He was also offered weekend work in Boots shops, which helped Derek's father, who was finally able to move to a better house with Joan.

Derek continued to be moved around to many different branches so that he gained more experience. From the first interview with Mr Gough to the kindness of Mr Cronk, Derek had been spotted as a young man with great potential. He had regular reviews, had to sit tests and was trained thoroughly. Boots was a solid, paternalistic employer and if he was willing to stick with them, then they would stick with him too. They explained that they hoped he would eventually become a qualified pharmacist, which meant doing degree-level training, which would take six years.

Although his family's circumstances had denied him the opportunity of going to university, Derek's father had been right to encourage him to better himself by getting to the grammar school. Derek's tenacity, love of learning and gratitude for any good treatment made him attractive to people, and his employers could clearly see in him a young man of great quality who could go far.

Nearing the end of his apprenticeship, Derek was serving in yet another Boots shop in Nottingham. His boss, Mr Kerry, was observing Derek very carefully one morning. At lunchtime Mr Kerry quietly said to Derek, 'Come wi' me, lad.'

Derek wondered what on earth he might have done wrong but, without a word, he obediently took off his white coat and followed Mr Kerry out of the shop. Another member of staff was left in charge and the two men walked in silence for a few minutes up the hill to a small park off the Derby Road. There was a little playground and church, and right slap bang in the middle of the park was a magnificent chestnut tree, with its regal spreading branches full of lush foliage. Derek and Mr Kerry stood looking up at the tree, from a few yards off, and Derek wondered what Mr Kerry was about to say. Had he got an order wrong? Had he killed a customer with bad pills? Derek racked his brain. His heart was racing and panic was rising. Was Mr Kerry going to fire him?

Finally, Mr Kerry spoke in a low voice, 'You see that tree, lad? Have a look at it.' Derek looked. 'A real look, mind.'

Derek looked again, very carefully. Indeed, they both stood looking at the tree for what felt like a good ten minutes. When Derek stopped and took in the tree, he saw that it indeed was a thing of wonder, a thing of mystery. He could see that behind it the sky was blue, with flecks of grey and huge white clouds. He took in the tree's full branches swaying against it, like an elegant dancing beauty, flashing her green fronds in all directions.

'You'll never see anything more beautiful in your whole life,' said Mr Kerry, with feeling.

They continued to stand for another few minutes in reverent silence and then Mr Kerry simply turned and started back up the road to the shop, and Derek followed.

6

Young Captain Happs

Christmas 1942 marked a significant turning point for nineteen-year-old Derek. Out of the blue, he was asked to join the Christmas dinner of the family of an attractive, bookish girl he had known at Ecclesfield Grammar School. He was loath to leave his father and young Joan, but Thomas said generously, 'Go on, Derek, we'll be fine, yer go and have some fun, son.' So that year Derek spent Christmas with another miner's family and their daughter, Denise, with whom he had sung in the choir and played tennis at school.

Denise's family's friends included a bus driver, Bob, and his wife, Madge, whom Dennis already knew from travelling on the local buses. They were warm, fun-loving people. The gathering was very amicable and lifted Derek's spirits. He missed his mother terribly at Christmas and, although his work at Boots was fulfilling and engaging, he always felt melancholy in the festive season, as it was all about family. So he was very grateful to be offered the chance to spend the festival with different people and to make new friends.

It was a jolly crew, and although the Christmas dinner was simple – a pork joint, roast potatoes and vegetables from the local plot and a homemade plum pudding – Derek felt incredibly grateful to be included at their family feast.

After lunch, shy Denise asked Derek to come and listen to the new Magnavox radiogram the family had acquired. The two young people went into the back room and she put on a record. It was cold in the room as there was no fire and they could see their breath steaming on the air. Denise put the needle down on 'The Star of Bethlehem', sung by the American tenor Frank Munn, whose voice filled the chill room with an intense, sweet sound. Derek was very musical and spiritual by nature, and he was also feeling heightened emotions, thinking about his mother. He listened intently to the song, sung with piercing emotion, side by side with Denise:

It was the eve of Christmas.
The snow lay deep and white,
I sat beside my window,
And look'd into the night,
I heard the church bells ringing,
I saw the bright stars shine,
And childhood came again to me,
With all its dreams divine.

As the song ended, Denise and Derek turned towards each other, looked into each other's eyes, almost mesmerised, and fell into each other's arms and kissed. All the pent-up feelings they had begun to brew for each other during the Christmas period were unleashed. They fell in love then and there. Indeed, from then on they played that record every Christmas, just to reconnect with the magical moment they 'saw' each other and fell in love.

By now, Derek was training with the army at Wakefield, and still working for Boots some weeks and weekends, as his apprenticeship did not finish until he was twenty. Derek and Denise became betrothed, although her father did not want them to marry until Derek was fully established at work – he wanted them to wait.

This was problematic for Derek, as he wanted to marry Denise as soon as possible as the war was on, but he understood and respected her father's doubts. The uncertainty of the war years meant that people often rushed into marriages due to impending separations or even just plain lust, and he could see that Denise's father wanted to ensure that his future son-in-law had the right motivations. Denise was his only daughter and so he was, naturally, a highly protective father.

Derek's full-time stint in the army tested their relationship further, but he wrote to Denise from wherever he was posted, and she wrote reams back. Her letters sustained him and gave him hope. Derek was posted to the Middle East, starting in Cairo with the Royal Engineers, and he saw action in the desert.

Derek witnessed a lot of terrible things during his time in the army, but his upbringing had given him an amazing capacity for endurance. He had developed the ability to deal with hardship, mixed with a huge dollop of compassion. Derek was a good soldier and became a good leader of men, rising eventually to the rank of captain and running an office in the middle of the desert by the time he was demobbed.

After the war, Derek finished off his engineering diploma in Wakefield and then was posted to a new job with Boots in Lincoln. He asked to be transferred to engineering within Boots, as he wanted to continue in that field. However, Boots's management wanted Derek to stick to pharmacology.

Derek, now ready to marry Denise and start a family, considered his options. He felt loyal to Boots, and grateful to the chances he had been given. Boots had become a household name across the nation, and was still growing. There was a shop on nearly every high street in the UK, and the management had its sights on starting overseas branches.

On his return to work, his previous Boots boss called him in for a review meeting. 'How's it been, Derek?' asked Mr Fisher, now in his sixties and heading for retirement. 'Seen some action, eh?'

'Oh, I'm fine,' said Derek, modestly. 'Just getting used to civvie street again.'

They laughed. Mr Fisher looked at a letter on his desk, and then up at the good-looking, tanned young man before him.

'Derek, I obviously don't know what you have planned, but I expect you know that you are only two years away now from finishing your qualification in pharmacology. This would mean that you'd be accepted into the Royal Pharmaceutical Society as a member. You'd be a qualified pharmacist, which would be equivalent to a degree, and you'd be able to dispense drugs yourself.'

Derek thought about it for a moment: he did like the idea of completing what he had started, way back in his first job, and he was aware that things were going to change quite a lot, post-war. A new health act was coming in, which would set up a National Health Service to provide free medicine to people who couldn't afford it. For Derek, this was a vocational call.

'I can see you have done very well for yourself during the war,' continued Mr Fisher. 'Boots would like to retain your services, and frankly, we think you will be offered a management role in the not-too-distant future, if you stay with the firm.'

Derek was amazed and thrilled. At that time, Boots divided itself up into a number of territories and was run in a fairly strict top-down fashion. However, it meant that everyone in the hierarchy knew exactly where they were and how things worked. Staff were tested and reviewed regularly to make sure that their knowledge was up-to-date, and as the company believed in quality control, it was willing to invest in training people.

Derek decided on the spot that he wanted to stick with Boots.

'Thank you, Mr Fisher,' he said, after a few moments. 'I'd be delighted to stay and finish my pharmacy training.'

7

Married Life

Derek and Denise married and very soon afterwards started a family. Derek finished his pharmacology exams with flying colours and became a fully fledged pharmacist and a member of the Royal Pharmaceutical Society.

'Ahm incredibly proud of you, son,' said Thomas, who had now retired as a miner, but was working still in Hoyland Common, packing boxes in a local factory. His body could no longer cope with going down the mine daily, as it was such a punishing job. He was still preaching for the Methodist Church, still spreading the Lord's word, wherever or whenever he could.

Derek felt proud to be able to dispense the first NHS prescription in Nottingham in 1950 when the new health act came into force. It was important for him to be able to help ordinary people improve their health and well-being. Having seen his mother die in so much pain, and so young, relatively speaking, Derek was highly motivated to relieve pain and suffering whenever and wherever he could.

Derek worked hard and gained a reputation within the company for being a fair yet firm manager. He had a kind, intelligent demeanour that evoked trust in people. He also had the ability to increase sales and productivity. His profits doubled and he was able to motivate staff to work hard and to increase their knowledge, while enjoying their work. Being able to serve people with courtesy and giving the customer what they wanted was Derek's watchword, and he made it his personal duty to praise and reward the staff's good behaviour whenever he could. Of course, there were times Derek had to sack staff, which was always a difficult task, but he was tough on their behaviour while respecting the staff member as a human being. This fine distinction got him far.

In 1950, Derek had just completed a successful three-year stint in Sheffield. He would move on to run a branch in Lincoln, then London and Southampton, helping turn each shop into a profitable business. At that time, Boots chemists dispensed late into the night. The shop was open seven days a week, and staff were on a rota from nine in the morning until they closed at eleven. The new NHS system was proving popular, and people could now register with a GP and get a written prescription and take it into Boots to be filled. There were still plenty of private doctors, as before, and there was a separate private prescription book that had to be filled out and checked by the pharmacist – now Derek.

One night there was a power cut, and Derek was alone in the pharmacy until eleven. There had been another staff member there, but Derek had just sent him home. It was a dark winter night, and the only light came from candles in the dispensary and a hand-held torch, the rest of the shop was in eerie darkness. Although the world was relatively safe and people were trusting, Derek was aware that he should keep his ears and eyes open for anyone wanting to come in and steal.

Suddenly, a craggy-faced man loomed up in front of Derek and absolutely terrified him. He was bald, with a fierce, muscular face and had eyes deeply sunk into his head. Derek stood at the counter, in the near darkness, and asked, 'Can I help you, sir?' and tried to stop his knees from knocking. The man had a strong malevolence about him and Derek felt he had to keep his wits.

'I want something to put my wife to sleep,' the man said, with a deep, sonorous voice that made Derek very uncomfortable.

He was taken aback. 'Ah, do you mean your wife is finding it hard to sleep?'

'No,' said the man, menacingly, 'I want to put her to sleep.'

Derek had to think fast. Was he about to murder his wife? 'Let me go and check something,' he said retreating into the back office to gather his thoughts. The best thing he could do was give him a mild preparation with something in it like valerian, which was used for insomnia. He had a feeling that this man was asking for chloroform or some other kind of sleep-inducing anaesthetic, and that would never be possible.

Derek emerged from his pharmacist's lair with a little brown-stoppered bottle. 'This should do the trick.'

'What is it?' asked the man, gruffly.

'Valerian,' explained Derek. 'I've made a mixture to help your wife sleep.'

'How much should she take?'

'Just two teaspoons,' said Derek, knowing he had made a fairly mild formula.

The man paid and left abruptly, leaving Derek feeling very shaken up by the whole event.

The next day, as Derek was reading the local newspaper, he saw a picture of the very same man: Boris Karloff. It was an advert, with his picture: the film star had a lead role in a new play at the local theatre. Derek remembered that he had recently been to the cinema and seen a frightening Dracula film starring Boris Karloff, and realised that was why he had found him so oppressive. He had had the dubious pleasure of serving a sleeping draught to Count Dracula.

8

Success and Beyond

From his humble and impoverished beginnings as a miner's son, Derek's professional journey had put him in charge of Boots branches, not only throughout the UK, including London, but abroad as well.

Denise supported Derek every inch of the way, as did their children, by moving house many times, even to New Zealand, when Derek was put in charge of opening the first Boots branch in that country. Boots rewarded Derek at every turn for his loyalty.

At one conference, Derek met the lofty chief pharmacist superintendent, Donald Sparsholt, who sought Derek out in a coffee break and said to him, 'When I retire I will appoint you as my successor.'

Derek worked his way through the Boots hierarchy to eventually become a director. The constant love, support and encouragement from his family was central to his ultimate success in life. He always stuck to his Methodist principles and the honourable manners and kindly behaviours he had learned from his beloved parents.

Derek had a direct and sensitive way with people, putting them at ease and yet, remembering his poor beginnings, never pulling rank. He managed to get the best out of himself and others, and his sales figures doubled due to his attitude of sincerity and integrity coupled with honesty and vision.

In 1967 he went to the Montreal World Fair representing Boots, and went to live with Native Americans, learning about their healing, medicines and Shamanic work. He also met Prince Philip twice, who even cheekily called Derek the 'Archbishop of Boots'.

He retired at sixty, with a sense of having achieved success, and travelled the world with his beloved wife. Her eventual death caused him enormous grief.

To this day, Derek is a campaigner and voice of Boots, and works with the archive to keep its history alive. At ninety-three he still enjoys his daily walk and plays the organ occasionally. Family is still the most important thing to him and he loves being with them, especially his seven grandchildren. He reads poetry, listens to music and tries to promote health and well-being wherever he goes.

Betty Allsop
née Nichols

Betty (second on the left) at the seaside in Skegness.

1

Disaster Strikes

While Derek Happs' family was determined to help him make the best of his life despite their gruelling poverty, little Betty Nichols was not going to be so lucky. In 1928, the year all women finally got the vote, Betty's impoverished family was living on Ransome Avenue in a tightly packed area of red-brick terraces known as the Meadows, situated in the south of Nottingham city centre alongside Nottingham Canal, leading down to the River Trent, which often flooded. Despite its leafy, pleasant name, the Meadows was a notoriously unhealthy, tough working-class area, packed with warehouses, factories and artisan dwellings.

The Nichols, comprising of mother, Sophia, twenty-six, and father, Sydney, twenty-nine, and Dorothy, nine, Morris, five, and little Betty, two, lived on the bottom floor of an airless two-up two-down, with a sewage trench or midden at the end of a tiny brick yard out the back. Sydney worked as a fireman on the railway and Sophia used to be a cleaner, but now was at home full time looking after the children and the flat.

One freezing, foggy night in November, there was a knock at the door. Dorothy, a child older than her years with a brown bob, opened it, only to find an enormous policeman looming over the doorstep. 'Yer mother needs to come to the 'ospital, right now,' he told the astounded Dorothy. 'There's no time to waste.'

'What is it, Dorothy?' asked Sophia, approaching the door anxiously, with a deep frown crumpling her handsome, thin face. She was holding Betty, a little girl with curly blond hair, on her hip, half-balanced on top of a huge bump bulging under her red floral dress. Betty had never seen a policeman up close before, and stared up at him, open-mouthed, as he removed his helmet and tucked it under his arm.

In an era before mass telecommunications, the only way to get an emergency message out to someone was for it to be delivered in person, and the police were usually the unfortunate messengers. PC Entwistle, as he told them to call him, had a bristly ginger moustache that twitched as he spoke. 'It's yer husband, Mrs Nichols, 'e's teken bad. Yer've to come now.'

By then, Morris was also at the door, and Mother handed Betty over to Dorothy, who plonked her down on the cold green lino floor. Perplexed, little Betty put her index finger in a curl and started twirling it, put the thumb of her other hand in her mouth and, sucking hard, began crying. 'There, there ...' said Dorothy, kindly, then

Morris started wailing, and soon the two smaller children were holding on to either side of their kindly big sister while their mother fetched her worn bottle-green coat and black cloche hat.

The freezing air was filling the downstairs room with night chill, so Dorothy and her tiny crying bookends shuffled backwards, and the policeman came in and closed the door. He almost filled up the lamp-lit room with his giant, black-uniformed presence, which cast an eerie dark shadow on the wall. The children watched intently as their mother carefully put her hat on with a pin, then straightened her chestnut fringe in a small cracked mirror on the wall over the butler sink and wooden drainer. Her face was chalk white, Betty noticed, and her lips were quivering.

Both Betty and Morris had quietened down by now and were wondering what on earth was going on. Their father had been in Nottingham General Hospital for the past week, and they knew he was poorly. But Mother had said that he would be home soon. Betty noticed the policeman's big boots with huge round toecaps, and thought they were smooth and shiny, just like Father's. Father! With that thought, Betty felt cold inside, like she couldn't breathe and she wanted to cry again. Where was Father ... her daddy?

'Ahem,' said PC Entwistle. He had got out his silver pocket watch on its long chain and was checking the time. Morris went over to him and peeked shyly at the watch face, then up at the policeman's face, fascinated by both. 'Mrs Nichols, are yer set?'

Betty watched her mother move as if in a dream as she buttoned up her coat over her big bump with some difficulty, then picked up her battered brown handbag. 'Listen to our Dorothy, children,' she said in a low whisper. 'Be good.'

'Ahm 'ungry ...' piped up Morris.

'Shh,' said Dorothy. 'Ah'll sort summat.'

The three children followed their mother and PC Entwistle to the door and watched her waddle off down the gas-lit cobbled street, a diminishing round figure, barely keeping up with the policeman's long stride. Quite a few women neighbours were now on their doorsteps, arms folded over their aprons, watching impassively. A policeman's visit was always noticed as nothing was secret in the Meadows: everyone knew everyone's business. Or, at least, tried to.

Betty started crying again, as she wanted her mummy, she wanted her daddy, it all felt terribly wrong. Morris joined in, both beside themselves. Dorothy played mother. 'It's all right m'ducks, it'll be all right ...' she said, leading them back into the gloomy room by their hands. 'Let's see what we've got in't cupboards.'

*

By the time PC Entwistle and the heavily pregnant Sophia reached the men's medical ward in the elegant and wealthy part of the city near Nottingham Castle, Sydney was dead. Sophia was distraught at not having been with her beloved at the very end. Staff Nurse Green pulled the metal-framed curtain screen on wheels around the bed to give her some privacy with her now cold husband. The long ward housed thirty beds, and most of the men were tucked up sound asleep, although there were occasional moans and groans, observed by a nurse on duty, who was sitting at a table with a light on, at the end of the ward.

Sophia sat and touched her husband's icy, stiffened hand, then she kissed it, shocked by its unresponsiveness. She could feel her baby turning round and round inside of her as she sobbed quietly into the pale green counterpane. How could he be gone? So soon? Only ten days ago he had been large as life in their tiny kitchen, eating her hotpot and telling stories about his day in the depot to the children. It was true he'd had a terrible cough and a fever, but surely he wasn't sick enough to die? He was so full of life, he was a good father and a loving husband, and now he was gone. Forever.

Sydney had survived the First World War, despite being injured in the trenches, and that was only a decade ago. He still had the shrapnel scars on his legs and arms to show his dedication to King and Country. He had spent months in this very same hospital recuperating after the war, and now he was taken by something as ordinary as a chest infection.

'It turned to pneumonia,' Sister had said, simply. 'There was nothing we could do.'

Ironically, this was the year that penicillin was discovered, but it would be a long time until it was available for general use. Until then, people would continue to die of cuts, wounds, chest infections – anything where bacteria could take hold.

Sydney had worked long hours on the railway and was a devoted husband and father, but they were poor and Sophia felt utter despair, as her baby moved inside her, reminding her that life would have to go on.

'It's a rum do,' whispered PC Entwistle sadly to Staff Nurse Green behind the screen. 'Them poor little 'uns.'

Both professionals were used to seeing such scenes daily, especially during the General Strike in 1926, which had hit working people extremely hard, but they were nonetheless touched to see such a young woman, especially in her current state, so bereft.

Staff Nurse Green was holding a package wrapped in brown paper, and moved the screen aside to hand it to Sophia. 'His belongings,' she said simply.

Outside, in the night air, Sophia walked back down the hill towards Old Market Square, clutching the brown paper parcel to her, weeping openly. She walked home as if underwater. Floating across the square, down Friar

Lane and Castle Road, through ever-narrowing streets towards the Meadows, filled with a gathering sense of dread as she got closer to home. How would she afford to bury her Sydney with the baby nearly here? There could be no headstone, surely. Maybe not even a proper funeral? How would she feed her family and manage things without her husband's weekly pay packet with a new babe in arms? He was a good man, and although he went to the pub, he never drank away his wages, like so many men in the Meadows. How would she fetch coal, mend things, manage? Tears flowed slowly down Sophia's cheeks as she stumbled home, mumbling and sobbing to herself, in a deepening state of shock and panic.

Once home, the brown paper packet lay on the scrubbed wooden kitchen table. Betty looked at it, confused. It wasn't Christmas yet, and there was no postman at night. It was way past midnight, way past their bedtime, and everything seemed topsy-turvy.

Mother sat looking blankly at the parcel, then at the children. Eventually she said, slowly, 'Father's not comin' home. Not ever.'

The children held their breath, almost too exhausted and frightened to cry any more, as Mother reached out slowly and pulled the paper parcel gingerly apart. Out fell Father's mash can – a white enamel flask for his tea and milk – followed by his snap box and his heavy black rubber-covered torch. Dorothy lifted his big black boots onto the floor, and Betty could almost hear her mother chiding her father, 'Tek them muddy boots off,' as she always did when he came home at night. He always undid his laces, good-naturedly winking at Betty and ruffling Morris's hair. Then she'd see her parents kiss hello and embrace warmly, looking into each other's eyes and laughing, which made her feel snug and safe inside.

Sophia lifted out his heavy cotton shirt and buried her face in it, then doubled over the table howling like a wounded animal, while the children huddled together terrified. Dorothy held both children to her as Betty started crying again: she loved her father's smell, of oil and coal and smoke. She loved him picking her up and feeling his strong shoulders under his rough black jacket. She even liked his whiskery face that was like a shorn hedgehog. She wanted her daddy back, she wanted him to give her a kiss and tell her a story at bedtime, like he always did, before all three children snuggled down into one bed, head-to-toe, like sardines.

Morris got under the table and hid, his favourite place in the house, especially in times of trouble – he felt much safer there.

'Yer've got to eat summat,' said Mrs Kimberley, Sophia's mother, chastising her daughter who lay on the bed like a corpse, facing the wall. 'Ah've brought yer some Bovril.'

Sophia didn't move.

'Yer've got to keep yer strength up, m'duck. Fer't baby's sake.'

At the mention of the baby, Sophia rolled over and sat up, her hair and clothes quite dishevelled, took the beef tea with trembling hands, and sipped.

Mrs Kimberley, who the children fondly called Nan, had come as soon as she could after the terrible news. A warm, bustling woman, she told the children she would stay until the baby came, but she said, 'Yer've all going to do your bit, to help yer mother.' Neighbours had rallied, bringing in bits of coal, half loaves and pots of hot food, or whatever they could spare. Old Mr Norris from down the road brought in soil-encrusted potatoes and carrots from the local allotment, and Nan got Morris and Dorothy peeling and scraping. Nan also helped with the practical matters and arranged a simple funeral. Luckily, Nan discovered that Sydney had paid a weekly amount to the Co-op to help with funeral costs through the railway company, and although there wasn't enough for a headstone, there would be enough money for a basic burial in St George's, the local parish church. To keep things going, Nan made bread, meat pie and Victoria sponge, blacked the grate with Zebrite, or polished the front door step red with Cardinal, and swept the floor, while Sophia lay semi-comatose, hardly eating and crying constantly.

Little Betty felt the world had ended. She clung on to Dorothy, watching her mother lie in bed, lifeless and pale, and feared what would happen to them all.

Then, one day, soon after her father's death, there was a knock at the door, and a plain pine coffin was brought in and propped up on two chairs, beside Sophia and Sydney's marital bed.

Sophia and her mother washed down Sydney's body very tenderly, as was the custom at the time, and prepared him for his burial. He was dressed in his best Sunday suit and shirt, wearing his braces and boots, and little Betty watched from across the room at all the comings and goings with bowls of water, bars of soap and brushes. Eventually, holding Dorothy's hand, she crept forwards to the coffin and peeked in. There was her father. His face. It was him, but it wasn't him at the same time. He looked so familiar, but now he looked grey and strange, with his cheeks and eyes all sunk in, like an ancient doll. But he was peaceful, and it was quiet in the flat, and the whole family sat round Father in all his finery, as if he was going to church on Sunday or to a wedding. Betty went up on tiptoe and put out her forefinger and touched his face and it was icy and hard. Like stone. Her daddy. She didn't like it, but it wasn't really frightening; it was just so strange.

Sophia sat lifeless on the edge of the bed with her face gaunt and pale. Meanwhile, Nan sat at the kitchen

table doing paperwork, applying to the railway company's hardship fund for widows. She also helped to release
Sophia's pension from them, although ten shillings a
week was not going to stretch very far at all. There was
no welfare state yet and most poor people feared ending
up in the dreaded workhouse, which still existed at the
time in some places, so Sophia knew she would soon have
to get paid work, despite the baby being imminent.

Even before the funeral, Nan insisted that life return
to some semblance of normality, and Dorothy and Morris
were sent back to their local primary school in Bosworth
Road. The school was full of poor children with parents
with TB, or maybe with typhoid or diphtheria, and
those who were unemployed, with no food on the table
or shoes to wear. Nan believed the best way to deal with
life's worries was to get on with things, as if nothing had
happened. That's what she'd had to do during the war,
when she was a 'clippie' on the buses. So Dorothy and
Morris were distracted, at least during the day, while
Betty stayed at home with her grief-stricken mother and
kind-hearted nan.

Two weeks after the funeral, Sophia went into labour
and the local midwife was called. Nan boiled water and
warmed towels, and together they helped little Dennis
arrive in the world. He was a lovely little baby with tufts
of dark hair, and he looked very like Sydney, which was
a strange comfort. 'Yer can hold 'im if yer like,' said

Mother, and the children took it in turns to cradle him and play with his little fingers and toes.

Nan stayed on for another two weeks, helping Sophia with the children and housework, but soon had to return home as her own husband was ailing. Betty sat sucking her thumb and watched her mother feed the new baby, but with such a forlorn face. Mother never smiled any more, never gave her cuddles or even seemed to notice her. She was often bad-tempered and snappy, and the baby cried and cried all the time. Betty felt it was miserable.

Dorothy stayed home from school to help, and Betty would go to her if she needed anything. Her mother seemed a strange, distant person, and Betty didn't want to worry her with anything. Every time she looked at Dennis she thought sad thoughts, like he would never know his daddy. Her daddy. Their daddy. The thought of her father, lying quietly in his coffin, looking all cold, grey and funny, would come back and haunt her, especially at night, like he was a ghoul. It all seemed like a dream. Why couldn't life go back to normal? Where did people go? Dorothy said Daddy was in Heaven, but where was that? Nan said the Lord looked after his own. But if God was good, why had he taken her lovely daddy away? Betty longed for Daddy to clump into the kitchen just one more time and tell a funny story about the workmen or the trains and his day down the depot.

Now it was all so quiet and heavy at home and at night she could hear the endless sound of crying, from both her mother and the new baby, that came from her parents' room.

2

Trying to Learn

Three years later in 1931, Betty was now at primary school, in a class of over forty children, struggling to keep up. The nation as a whole was in crisis, and a National Government was set up with the three main parties, led by Ramsay MacDonald, the ex-Labour prime minister, to try ease unemployment and poverty. Although a bright child, Betty was struggling to keep up at school. Not only was she often kept home from school to help her mother out with the housework, she also found it hard to spell and found her letters difficult to write. She had what would today be called dyslexia or a learning difficulty, but then such problems were understood as being 'stupid' or 'lazy'.

Miss Pennyweather, a strict and bloodless teacher in a tight grey suit, had little time for the small, quiet child at the back of the class. Betty was often picked on by the bigger children and resorted to hiding in the outside lavatories across the playground to avoid the bullies. She would walk home at lunchtime for a slab of bread and dripping or a sugar sandwich and sometimes just didn't go back. 'Fetch us some fuel could yer?' her mother might ask, plaintively, and Betty would run off dutifully to collect coal dropped by the rail track or by a cart or truck, or to find kindling for the fire.

Betty would wander around the Meadows to the cricket pavilion (built by Jesse Boot, the founder of Boots, for workers to enjoy), or along the Victoria Embankment by the First World War memorial, where trees shed their leaves. Keeping the range going was essential for the family's welfare, but buying coal was expensive. Sophia worked as a cleaner in a local hosiery factory, often taking Dennis with her, or asking old Mrs McKeown down the road to sit with him for an hour or two.

By now, Dorothy was working at a local embroidery factory in the Meadows, but Morris was just going up to big school and baby Dennis would be going to infants fairly soon. Dorothy came home on a Friday night and put her wages in a red Oxo tin in the kitchen. She never complained, but her life was a round of work and sleep and any spare time was spent helping at home. Mother was often crying, or was exhausted and needed help. Sophia taught Betty to cut down dresses and 'make do and mend' as much as possible, and Betty found she was quite skilled with her needle and thread.

Typically, Monday was washday, and Betty was often kept at home off school to help while Dorothy was out earning vital extra shillings. 'Get the copper in, Betty,' her mother would say first thing, and Betty would bring in a large pan with handles from the yard and set it on the range. Sophia and Betty would fill it with buckets of water, add Omo or Sunlight soap flakes, then heat it to boiling and put in the washing, bit by bit, pummelling it clean with a 'ponch' – a wooden stick with a round half cup on the end with holes, through which the water escaped like a little colander. If it was a whites-only wash then a little bag of Reckitt's Blue would be added to brighten them up. Anything that was to be starched, such as collars, were dunked in dissolved Robin crystals and hung out to dry. The washing became very heavy once it was sodden, so a pair of wooden tongs were used to help lift the laundry out of the copper. 'Gi' it some elbow grease, girl,' Sophia would encourage, and Betty would scrub away as hard as she could at filthy collars and white socks, or shirts and underwear, with a block of carbolic soap and a bristle brush on a wooden, ridged washboard, which was set on the drainer.

The washing had to be put through a mangle afterwards to squeeze out the excess water, which meant pulling large quantities of heavy, dripping material out of the copper across to the sink and into the mangle. Bedsheets, counterpanes, curtains and tablecloths were a two-woman job. 'Come 'ere, lass, and get hold of t'other end,' her mother would command Betty, and the child would feed a mass of sodden white material through the mangle, sometimes two or three times, as her mother wound the handle round and round and round, getting very red in the face with the effort. Soon the room would be filled with masses of steam, suds and the smell of soap.

Finally, the washing was hung out, dripping, when the weather was fine, either across the street, on a thick string line, or across the tiny backyard, but the whites often came in again fairly grey, with specs of soot scattered across them. When the weather was wet, washing was strung around the living room, steaming in front of the range, over doors, over the chairs, hanging on any ledge, and exuded a damp, soapy atmosphere for days. Both Sophia and Betty had red, cracked hands after wash day, which, in the winter, led to dry, split skin, dermatitis and chilblains.

After the washing came the ironing, something every self-respecting woman had to do. 'Fetch the flatiron, Betty,' Sophia would say, and the child lifted a heavy, cast-iron implement from the floor to the top of the black range to heat it up. The washing was then pressed on the wooden kitchen table, emitting yet more steam, as it was still damp. This was sometimes quite a dangerous job, as the one ironing would inevitably burn their hands; a livid painful patch appearing on their skin the second they brushed up against the hot iron. Sometimes clothes ended up with a brown scorch mark from leaving the iron on them too long. Betty's arms would ache as she ironed a sheet, which seemed endless, then folded it carefully with her mother and put it to 'air' over the range on a wooden rack dryer.

3

Happy Again

In 1936 King George V died, after twenty-six years on the throne and the nation went into official mourning. Black bunting was hung across streets, black material was wrapped around lampposts, shops and vehicles; at home, people draped black respectfully over pictures of the dearly departed King and wore black armbands to mark their personal loyalty. His son, Edward VIII, took over, but his reign was to be short-lived, as he would abdicate by December of that year to live in scandalous exile in France with Mrs Wallis Simpson, an American divorcée.

The country had swung to the right the year before, when Stanley Baldwin took over from the National Government, but the economy was still shaky, although recovering very slowly.

In September 1936, Betty was to go up to 'big' school, the grandly named Queen's Walk School for Girls. Betty still struggled to keep up with her schoolwork, not only due to her reading difficulty, but also down to her having missed quite a lot of school. At home, Morris was now working as a plumber's apprentice at Roper's, a family business in Willoughby Street. It was a good job, although the pay was poor, so the family was still struggling financially. And things were about to change for the better, as their mother had been smiling again of late.

'Ah want yer to meet Arnold,' mother had announced one summer's evening, much to everyone's surprise. Betty and Dorothy were mending clothes at the table, Dennis was on the floor, playing with a wooden puzzle, and Morris was in the yard, mending a chair, when a pleasant-looking man in a tweed jacket and cap came to the front door. Arnold Atkins was taller than Mother, with a muscular build, a kind, open face, plentiful dark hair and twinkly brown eyes. When he entered the cramped room, he took off his cap and smiled. 'Ayup, you must be Dorothy and Betty.'

The girls looked up from their mending and Betty found herself feeling quite shy.

'Say hello,' prompted Mother, somewhat embarrassed.

'Hello,' chimed both girls shyly, in unison.

'And that's our Dennis,' said Mother, pointing to the floor. But Dennis was absorbed in his puzzle and ignored them. 'Sit yersel' down,' said Sophia, and she got a bottle of Home Brewery stout out of her bag and opened it for Arnold, handing him the bottle and a glass.

By now, Morris was standing at the back door, watching the scene. Dorothy and Betty looked at each other in surprise, and then back at Arnold and their mother, then at Morris, and wanted to giggle. Mother took off her coat and hat, hung them on the peg on the door, then cleared her throat and looked at the floor. Suddenly she said, 'Arnold works in't Royal Ordnance Factory, here in't Meadows. Anyway,' she paused, 'we're gettin' wed.' The girls' jaws dropped. 'Next Saturday,' said mother, before they could object. 'Yer'll both be bridesmaids,' she added quickly, 'Nothing fancy.'

Betty didn't know what to say, but Dorothy looked bemused, and then said, for them both, 'Ahm 'appy for yer, Ma.'

Morris looked amazed and shrugged, while Dennis still worked on his puzzle, ignoring them all.

Arnold took a gulp of beer and then joined in, 'Yer mother and ah've been courting this past six month, and, well …' he paused looking up at Sophia whose cheeks were now flushed deep pink, as she beamed at him, '… well, we want to mek a go of it. Together, like.'

Betty could see her mother's obvious happiness and suddenly she felt lighter inside, like a dark cloud had been lifted. 'Congratulations,' she said, and she meant it with all her heart.

Arnold was a warm, kind-hearted man and with him in their lives things began to get better and better.

After the wedding he came to live in the house with them all and Betty thought she'd never seen her mother looking prettier or more at ease. That summer and autumn they all went down to Trent Bridge for a picnic and even a game of cricket a couple of times. They'd never had days out or a holiday before, so taking a basket with pork pies, home-grown tomatoes (Arnold had green fingers at the allotment), and a chunk of cheese and bread, washed down with a bottle of Home Brewery Light Ale for the grown ups or R. White's cream soda, was utter bliss.

One drowsy afternoon, Betty lay back on the grass for a rare moment of relaxation and watched the white puffs of cloud scudding fast overhead. She listened to the birds tweeting away in the trees, the sound of children's voices laughing in play and the thrum of adult conversation. For a moment the world stood still as Betty chewed on a sweet grass stem with the sun falling on her face and the comfort of the warm earth beneath her body, holding her firmly. She felt happy, an unusual experience. If only life could be like this all the time. They had more money now with Arnold's wages, and they had more fun, as Arnold was with them. They'd all had new shoes, more fresh food and the flat had had a lick of paint. Arnold was a good singer, and would come into the kitchen singing 'Oh, I Do Like to Be Beside the Seaside' or some other popular or silly song, like 'The Teddy Bears Picnic', and

Sophia would fall about laughing. Mother was making dresses for them, and baking cakes and puddings, and it seemed like life was finally looking up.

Betty was now twelve, going on thirteen, and she knew she would have to start thinking about what job to go for. Both Dorothy and Morris had started work at thirteen, and she knew she would soon be facing that decision.

Little did Betty know that afternoon under the summer trees that disaster was about to strike for a second time. Unlike lightning, it seemed that bad things could happen, twice in a row, in the same place, and hurt their little family, with impunity. Only eighteen months after they married, Arnold became ill, quite rapidly, and retreated to bed. He developed a high fever, and Sophia's face became grey and tight all over again.

Arnold went into a sudden decline, and from being a robust, muscly man, thwacking a cricket ball with a bat, or throwing little Dennis up in the air in play, he became a wretched pile of skin and bone. The doctor shook his head when he saw him eventually, and Arnold was diagnosed with typhoid and sent straight off to the isolation ward at the hospital. He was very sick and sadly untreatable.

Betty was distraught, as were they all. She had got used to having a father figure around and life with Arnold in it had been light, lively and fun. Her mother visited Arnold nightly in the hospital until he died, and they all watched as their mother returned to the depressed wretch she had been before meeting her new husband. Again the family was facing life without a man. Betty felt life was cruel, and that men just didn't seem to last very long at all. By the time she left school at thirteen, without any certificates to her name, dear, funny Arnold was dead and buried and her mother was back to wearing black.

4

Hemming Shirts

About the same time as heartbroken, sixteen-year-old Derek was eating breakfast with Mr Cronk, his kindly Boots boss, about an hour north of Nottingham in south Yorkshire, little Betty, now thirteen, was walking along cobbled Traffic Street that wound through the Meadows. It was August 1939 and her first day of work, and even at seven in the morning, she was amazed to find the road was already buzzing with workers. There were people walking everywhere, many of them in clogs and boots, in hats and caps, many on bicycles and most, of course, like Betty, on foot. People seemed to be talking and chatting in a lively way, or mumbling and grumbling, or simply emitting smoke from their ubiquitous roll-ups, even at this time of the morning.

Eventually she stopped at an enormous, red-brick factory building and looked up several stories and along for as far as she could see: it seemed to go on for ever. The factory towered over her and she certainly felt intimidated. There was an arch leading on to an inner courtyard in the middle (which must have been where the horses and carts had gone in the old days, thought Betty), and over it, in black lettering, were the words that she could just about make out: 'The Cellular Clothing Co. Ltd'.

Betty swallowed hard, and felt very nervous indeed. The place looked very uninviting now she was this close up. She held on tight to her homemade shoulder bag (which she'd adapted from an old floral skirt) and which held her dinner of a bread and dripping sandwich that she had wrapped in greaseproof paper. Luckily she remembered to go round to the staff entrance, as she'd been instructed at her interview the week before, and joined the end of a long queue of women, all much older than her, walking rapidly towards it. There was a lot of pushing and shoving to get through the swing door entrance.

'Ayup, Ethel,' shouted one woman in bright red lipstick and a brown coat to another one in a green checked coat and red curls.

'Ayup, Marge, how do?'

'Summat rotten,' shouted Marge, and rolled her eyes, making Ethel laugh.

'It's Monday, int'it?' shouted Ethel back. 'What d'yer expect?' and Marge laughed heartily in return.

Betty flattened herself along the wall to let the regulars go past first in a swarm, then she latched on to the end of the fast-disappearing queue and ended up at an opaque glass window in the dingy reception area. The window was more like a hatch and Betty stood around, feeling very lost, not knowing what to do or where to go.

Suddenly the hatch opened, and a man's bodyless face appeared. 'Name!' he demanded.

'Betty Nichols,' said Betty, nervously.

'Wait on,' said the man and snapped the hatch shut.

Betty waited as more women streamed by her, chattering and laughing, and she retreated into a dark corner where she could watch things better. She noticed there was a strange grey machine in the other corner by the double doors, where the women were taking out rectangular pieces of brown card and putting them into a slot. There was a 'clunk-ping' and then they put it back into the wooden rack on the wall, next to a big clock.

'Right-oh, Nichols,' the man's voice was shouting across the hall at Betty, who suddenly realised he was talking to her. She went over to the hatch and waited. 'Yer've to go and find Elsie Dunn.'

'Oo's that?' whispered Betty.

'Elsie's your overseer,' said the man impatiently. 'In't finishing shop. Don't you know owt?'

With that, the hatch shut abruptly, leaving Betty standing staring at it none the wiser. She thought about knocking on the hatch, but the man seemed very angry. So Betty decided to walk along the corridor with the flow of women who were still arriving in twos and threes and see where they were all going. However, she didn't have a brown card to put in the strange clock machine, like they did, and she hoped to goodness she would soon understand what on earth she was supposed to do.

The noise was what hit her first. It was utterly deafening. Betty was standing in a vast room, the biggest she had ever been in, under an incredibly high ceiling with metal bars across it and lights dangling down on wires. There were rows and rows and rows of women sitting on high stools in front of strange metal rivers that were flowing past them, which were stopping, then starting, then stopping again, with a great clunk and crash. The women also all had in front of them what looked like treadle sewing machines. Luckily, Betty recognised what they were as they had an old Singer at home that she, her mother and Dorothy used a lot. The overall noise was how she imagined a hundred machine guns would sound if they were firing and making a racket in an empty aircraft hangar. She couldn't hear herself think.

'You new?' a woman snapped at her. 'Which department?'

Betty looked into the crinkly face of a woman with her hair tied up in a strange sort of scarf with a knot at the top. No hair was showing at all, but she had a pair of steel-rimmed glasses on. 'Y–y–yes, ahm Betty …' she said, scared to death, 'Ah've no idea where ahm to go.'

The woman produced a brown clipboard from behind her back and ran a stubby finger down the sheet on it, 'Betty … Betty, is it Nichols?'

Betty nodded, meekly.

'Right, come wi' me.'

Betty was taken through the double doors again, through to the staff reception where she'd come in in the first place. Betty noticed the hatch was still closed, but there were no workers coming in now.

'Right,' said the woman again, in her foghorn voice. 'Ahm Mrs Dunn, and ahm yer overseer.' Mrs Dunn looked down at Betty, who was small and thin for her age, quite scrawny but pretty. She opened a cupboard and fished out some garments. 'Go an' put these on, pronto,' she ordered, pointing to a door.

Betty scuttled off, holding on to them for dear life, and when she came back, Mrs Dunn thought Betty certainly looked like she was drowning in her grey overalls and headscarf.

Betty had tied the head scarf as well as she could, but Mrs Dunn redid it, 'No 'air's to show,' she barked, pushing wayward blond curls roughly out of sight. 'Basic rules. Listen carefully: yer to clock in in the morning, and if yer more than five minutes late, yer can go 'ome again.' Betty's eyes widened at this. 'Yer'll get no work that day if yer late. Not if yer want payin' any road. 'Undreds will tek yer job if yer not 'ere on' time.' Betty nodded vigorously at this edict. 'Then, Ah'll show yer yer machine – yer 'emming. Yer can sew, can't yer?'

Again, Betty nodded as hard as she could.

They started walking along the corridor, with Betty's overall flapping around her legs, 'No talking, no eating, no drinking at yer machine. No make-up, no earrings, no jewellery at all. No breaks, no going t'lavvy, and just half an hour fer yer dinner. Got it?'

Betty couldn't speak, all she could do was nod. She was following Mrs Dunn back through the double doors, and up some rickety, dimly lit cement stairs with open iron railings to the next floor. ''Emming,' said Mrs Dunn, and walked Betty along a long conveyor belt to where there was an empty seat. There was a table-like shelf sticking out at right angles to the conveyor belt with a sewing machine attached to it with a treadle underneath. This was Betty's workstation. The stool was a little high for Betty and she had a bit of a struggle getting on it. However, Mrs Dunn was a woman on a mission and shouted into Betty's right ear against all the noise. 'Yer ter wait until a piece of material comes along, an' yer tek it off, 'em it seam to seam, proper like, finish off – then put it back. Got it?' And with that she was gone.

Betty looked after Mrs Dunn for reassurance, then Mrs Dunn looked back at her over her shoulder. 'Ahm watching you,' she shouted over the din. 'No monkey business.'

Betty sat for a moment, mesmerised by the conveyor belt that was juddering past loudly one moment and shuddering to a stop the next. The din of the workshop was unbearable, and all the women were bent over their workstations, feverishly machining their own little bit of material. No one looked up from her work. Betty watched the young woman to the left of her for a moment: she picked up a hemmed piece of shirt, and attached it to another piece of shirt and made a side seam. She got her second piece of shirt from a basket beside her sewing machine. Betty looked to the right of her, where another woman was sewing up the other side of the shirt, and attaching it to the front panel.

The woman on her right looked over at Betty, and shouted, 'Ahm Ena.' Betty nodded at her grateful for some human contact, 'Yer ter 'em this bit when it comes to yer.' She put her piece on the conveyor belt and it started off towards Betty. 'Pick it up,' shouted Ena. Dutifully, Betty picked it up and held the piece of white-and-blue striped shirt. The material felt nice and expensive, like nothing she had ever handled before.

'What do ah do?' said Betty, almost panicking.

''Em it,' shouted Ena. 'From side seam to side seam.'

'No gossiping,' they heard suddenly, as Mrs Dunn loomed up behind Betty and Ena. 'Ah told yer no talking!'

Betty shrunk into herself. Thankfully, her machine was already threaded up with white cotton, so she folded over the edge of the material twice, very thinly, positioned the bottom hem of her piece of stripy material under the needle foot, lowered it, and treadled away with both feet (which only just reached if she perched on the edge of her stool), hemming from one side to the other. Betty double-checked her stitching was straight and the stitches themselves were even – that meant the tension was fine for the material. She then finished off on either side by tying off the threads and knotting them.

'Speed up,' said Mrs Dunn, watching her over her shoulder. 'Yer'll have to be quicker than that.' Mrs Dunn took the sewing and inspected it closely. 'No knots,' she spat out. 'Only satin stitch as a seam finish.'

She handed Betty a garment which had a perfectly neat seam, finished off with a square of stitching in tight, even, satiny threads. Then Mrs Dunn indicated to Betty to put her completed piece back on the conveyor belt and hit a big green button on the side. The belt duly jerked into life and travelled along to the woman on her left, who picked it up. Betty's hemmed shirt-tail was then picked up and attached to the other front of the shirt. By the time her left-hand neighbour had picked up and hemmed her piece, her right-hand neighbour, Ena, had done the next piece, which was hurtling towards Betty. So Betty had to machine another hem all over again. That was the job. Hemming. From the right seam, to the left, round the bottom of the shirttail, and then finish off with a neat zigzag of satin stitching, characteristic of the brand.

5

Doing Yer Bit

The Cellular Clothing Company Ltd had been set up in 1888 by Lewis Haslam, a successful Victorian entrepreneur. The company had grown rapidly, and now had huge factories in Swindon, London and Nottingham. The Nottingham factory – and Betty's section – specialised in underwear and men's shirts, as well as Aertex sportswear for the military, schoolchildren and sportsmen and women. The shirts were sold to big branded companies, such as Van Heusen, but were essentially the same as shirts sold to other outlets. There were variations in design, although most of the shirts were white, grey or pinstriped.

Working hours were long, starting at 8am and ending at 5pm, with half a day on Saturday. And the working conditions were harsh. Music was not allowed and lighting was poor, with generally a single light bulb high up near the ceiling, at best. Workers were not allowed to get up and go to the lavatory or take a smoking break or get a drink without express permission from Mrs Dunn (it really had to be an emergency). There were strict demarcated break times, when tea was available from a trolley or workers drank from their own mash cans. Dinner was also taken just sitting on a step or hunkering down on a bit of kerb out the back.

Betty usually ran home the ten minutes to her house, where she could grab some bread and tea. Her mother worked as a cleaner still, but was sometimes at home, and Betty would inevitably get asked to do a chore of some sort while she was there. She didn't mind as she loved her mother and felt worried that she had had such a tough time in life, being a single mother of four and twice-widowed. Her mother was still quite sad a lot of the time, so Betty went home just to reassure herself that her mother was all right.

The Second World War was soon upon them, as was memorably announced by Winston Churchill on the wireless in September 1939, and although things seemed relatively peaceful for the first few months, Betty and her family all felt frightened. They received their gas masks and put tape on their windows to stop them blowing in during an air raid. Mother made blackout curtains for all the windows. When it came to shelters, they didn't have enough space out the back for their own, so they shared a communal one near their house.

Soon there was discussion about the children being evacuated. Morris, Betty and Dennis had been invited to stay with Aunty Maud in Keyworth, as it was seven miles south of the city centre and deemed far safer than the Meadows, especially as there was the munitions factory there that Arnold had worked in.

'Ah want you to go,' insisted Sophia one evening round the table.

But Betty said, 'No, ah want to stay with you, Ma.'

Morris, Dennis and Betty tried living with their aunty for a week, but they soon all beetled back to be at their mother's side. They were homesick, and didn't want to leave their mother and Dorothy on their own. In her heart of hearts, Sophia didn't want them to go either, and so it was decided, against all better judgement, that the family would stick together, come what may. Strangely, the family ate better now rationing was on, as they were allocated their rations of cheese, butter, meat and milk every week. They still supplemented it with turnips, swedes, carrots, potatoes and cabbages from the communal allotment Arnold had tended before he died.

The boys thought it was all a bit exciting, even when the first bombing raids started and they all had to make a dash to the local air-raid shelter in the middle of the night. Betty was frightened, but also found it all quite exciting, in a strange kind of way. Most evenings after work, the family sat indoors with the blackout curtains pulled across, listening to the radio or reading the local paper. Suddenly the air-raid siren would start its fearful wail and Sophia would say, 'C'mon, they're bombing,' and the family would scramble, grab their pyjamas and gas masks and head for the shelter.

It was scary, especially as they could hear the thumping, booming and whistle of shells all night along with the anti-aircraft fire. It was terrifying when the bombing was heavy or nearly overhead and the ground would shake like jelly.

In the morning, they would step out and see houses bombed out all around them, like tombstone teeth scattering the landscape, a disconcerting sight. There were even dead bodies on stretchers, covered with grey blankets, which haunted Betty as they reminded her of seeing her dead dad. Important landmarks in Nottingham disappeared, like the Moot Hall and St George's church. Even so, after losing their real father and the lovely Arnold, the family felt, without being able to put it into words, that they wanted to stick together, even at the risk of losing their lives.

Meanwhile, still at Cellular Clothing, Betty was now one of the girls. By fourteen she had learned to smoke, and at break time she would pop into the lavatory and have a surreptitious cigarette. It calmed her down. She had also made friends with Ena and Molly, the woman on her left. She had learned to hem and perfect the special 'Cellular Clothing' satin stitch sign off with ease.

One day, the girls in their section were all called to the canteen by Mrs Dunn. 'We're switchin' ter military shirts,' she explained. 'It's part of our war effort. If we don't get bombed out first.'

The girls laughed. Mrs Dunn could be funny sometimes.

Now Betty was sewing blue shirttail hems for the RAF and white shirttail hems for the army. She had got faster and faster, neater and neater, and could do her job in her sleep. She churned out seamed shirttail after seamed shirttail, often while day-dreaming about Clark Gable, having just seen *Gone with the Wind*, which was on at the Odeon, or imagining replacing Ginger Rogers and dancing with Fred Astaire.

The work was boring, boring, boring. It was the same thing day in and day out, but Betty was used to it now. She knew she had to bring in the money, and she felt she was doing her bit towards the war effort. Her mother was still sad a lot of the time, but Morris was now in the army and Dennis was finishing school. Dorothy worked in another factory nearby, which had swapped embroidery for war goods, and she was courting Freddie, a nice young man who was away fighting in the army, just like Morris was now.

6

Love is in the Air

Four years later, in 1943, the war was still raging, and life was getting tougher. Nottingham had had its fair share of bombing and destruction but, luckily, the Nichols were all still intact. Betty still worked at Cellular Clothing and still hemmed shirts, the blue RAF ones and the white army ones, day in, day out. She could often get through forty in a day. She had learned to get her head down and treadle fast, though Mrs Dunn still came round and chided anyone who popped their head up and tried to chat to beat the boredom.

Most weekends were spent at home, helping Mother make do and mend, but one weekend Betty visited her aunty Maud in Keyworth – the same kind aunty who had offered take them in for a safe haven at the beginning of the war. Betty was bored, and really needed a break. Living during wartime had now become normal to her, but still scary at times.

This particular weekend there was a family birthday get-together for Aunty Maud, and Betty was relieved to grab her gas mask in its khaki box and get on a green bus that trundled through the streets and past fields to get out of the city. How she welcomed the change of scene and the fresh air.

When Betty arrived there were some distant relatives there who she had never met before. Being shy, Betty hung back in the garden and looked at the flowers and then helped out her aunty handing round the almost comically flat and rather unappetising powdered-egg sponge cake, which was typical wartime fare.

As Betty was pouring tea she suddenly saw an eye-catching young man in a naval uniform standing by the window. Her heart turned over and she nearly dropped the teapot. She found herself staring at him and then blushed, as he noticed and came over to speak to her. Betty fumbled around with the milk and teapot, embarrassed.

'Hello,' he said, offering his hand. 'Ahm Arthur. And you are?'

Betty's cheeks were burning with shame, and she couldn't look up at his shining brown eyes. 'Ahm, er, ahm, er Betty,' she managed, and blushed even more, shaking his hand awkwardly.

Arthur looked bemused for a moment. 'Ah've not seen you 'ere before?'

'No,' said Betty. 'Ah don't see Aunty Maud that often, not since the war started.'

Betty soon found herself relaxing as Arthur was warm and friendly and asked her lots of questions about herself.

They soon established that they were, indeed, distant relatives, but had never met before. Arthur had joined the Royal Navy as soon as he could and had been away at sea for the past two years. He spoke at length about life on ship and Betty was enthralled. He was just an able seaman, but he looked stunning in his uniform and she made him laugh when she said she'd probably stitched his shirttails – he was genuinely impressed.

Betty and Arthur shared a bus back to Nottingham in the early evening and simply could not stop talking. Betty didn't want the bus journey to end, and when Arthur said, 'Can ah walk you 'ome?' she instantly said yes. He seemed a gentleman, and a gentle man, and she was amazed that he seemed actually interested in her. No one had ever paid her any attention before, especially not a handsome young man in uniform who seemed so worldly and yet kind.

Oh, she'd been to the Palais de Danse with her friends from work once or twice, but she'd just drunk a cream soda while the older girls had beer. She'd had a couple of sweaty dances with soldiers and local factory lads, but had escaped with her virtue intact. Betty was shy and quite delicate, and didn't like being pawed. The women at work were all older, and quite a few were married, so their conversation was often smutty, and Betty didn't like their crude ways. However, Arthur seemed different. He talked about his travels, his experiences at sea, books he'd read, films he'd seen, and he was warm and genuinely interested in her.

It seemed the feeling was shared, and after this meeting they decided to see each other whenever they could. Arthur was soon back at sea, steaming into battle, while Betty was at the conveyor belt, hemming for Britain, but her mind was now full of imagining lovely evenings holding hands, with tender kisses and cuddles, and marvellous moments of laughter and fun. She could think of nothing else except when she would see her wonderful Arthur again.

Mutually besotted, they wrote each other letters as often as they could, planning in great detail what they would do together once the evil Mr Hitler had been put in his place, for good.

7

Finding Love

After the war, Betty was still working at Cellular Clothing and still hemming her shirts on the conveyor belt from 8am to 5pm every day. Her family had survived the war, and in 1947 she finally married her dear, lovely Arthur in a small, quiet wedding, after he had been demobbed. They rented a two-up-two-down together on Cambria Street in St Ann's, in a fairly rough but affordable district. And thus Betty finally moved out of the Meadows, leaving her mother and younger brother Dennis behind. By then, Dorothy had married her Freddie and Morris had been demobbed and was working in the huge Boots warehouse in Beeston.

Arthur needed a job and found one through a relative in Keyworth, whose uncle ran Marshall's the plumbers. He had to learn new skills, but he was pretty adaptable and happy to have a job in civvie street. What's more, he was over the moon when Betty announced, nearly a year later, that she was 'in the family way'. Even so, Betty kept working as they needed the money.

After the war, the company had allowed her to continue her job, despite being married. It was a time of flux. She would have to stop work, however, once the baby came.

Betty was ecstatic. As she sat on the bus to work, and then walked up the cobbles of Traffic Street alongside her fellow workers early in the morning, she could feel the baby moving snugly inside her in that familiar whirling motion. She would clock in and go and put her overalls on and head for her usual work station in hemming.

'Morning Ena, Morning Mary,' Betty said as she heaved herself and her bump up onto her stool one day.

'Morning,' they replied in unison.

Molly had left to have a baby, and been replaced by Mary, although the rest of the workforce was fairly constant, give or take a few.

'Eeh, yer look like yer going to drop any minute,' quipped Ena.

'No talking,' snapped Mrs Dunn, hovering as usual behind them.

Betty settled to work, aware that she had to meet her daily rate which was now sixty shirt hems. Although they were back to civilian clothes, and it was the usual white, pale grey, and pinstripe (blue, grey, black), there were attached collars as a regular feature, so the job was a bit more complicated. The conveyor belt jumped into action and Betty found it difficult to heave her body over it to reach her piece of side-seamed material when it travelled towards her from Ena. It was getting harder and harder to perch on her stool and to reach across, and she wondered if she'd actually make it to the end of her pregnancy.

By then, Betty was seven months pregnant, nearly eight, and feeling good, or at least better than she had been. She had felt pretty sick and weary for the first three months and had had to get off her stool and run outside and be sick nearly every day, to Mrs Dunn's visible annoyance. But things had gradually settled down. She had found drinking ginger pop and having a dry ginger or arrowroot biscuit helped, keeping the latter with her in her overall pocket.

One day she had asked Mrs Dunn, although she was still quite wary of her, 'Ah feel sick a lot and need the toilet, so could ah go outside and eat my biscuit if ah need to?'

Mrs Dunn had looked irritated. This was exactly the problem of allowing pregnant women to continue to work on the factory floor. She really ought to be at home. It interrupted the flow. But Betty was a good girl, a quiet worker, who always got her head down to meet her quota, and didn't go outside and smoke cigarettes, pretending she was going to the lavatory, like so many of the girls. She never got any cheek or bad language from her either. The factory had become a bit laxer about letting girls go outside between official breaks, but it was still something Mrs Dunn kept her beady eye on.

'Go on wi' yer,' she had whispered. 'But don't tell anyone, else they'll all want special favours.'

Betty was discreet about their arrangement, and she would signal to Mrs Dunn when she came into view down her aisle and Mrs Dunn would nod her head and signal, 'Go on, be quick about it,' so Betty could get some relief.

Now on her stool, reaching over to pick up her next shirttail to hem, Betty thought about her baby. She was so happy with Arthur and had never thought she would be so harmonious and comfortable with someone. They had a quiet life together, reading the paper, listening to the wireless and, recently, decorating their bedroom and preparing a cot. Betty had knitted several matinée jackets, hats, mittens, pants, and a shawl in white and lemon-coloured wool (she'd got a job lot from the market). She didn't want to make them either in pink or blue, as she didn't want to get it wrong – so white and lemon seemed quite safe.

Arthur was a practical man, and they worked the allotment together; he dug up potatoes while Betty planted and cut flowers. She loved gardening and imagined she would bring their little one to dig and plant seeds. In her mind's eye, she imagined them growing big sunflowers, or Michaelmas daisies and anemones. She felt hopeful as the world was renewing itself, finally, despite all the destruction and pain of the war.

But she had noticed that her brother Morris was quite different since he had come home. He seemed morose and, although he never said anything, she sensed he'd had a very hard time in action. Many of the men she knew were like that, dark and depressed after the war, drinking their pints, but not saying very much. A lot of them had a difficult time settling back in. She was lucky, so lucky, that she had her Arthur, who wasn't unhappy, and after all the disruption of her childhood she was determined to make a go of building a happy family life. She was thankful her Arthur had come back to her intact and was faithful to her, unlike so many of the men who had gone away to war.

Two weeks later, at work, sitting on her stool, Betty was treadling away on her twentieth shirt hem of the day when there was an almighty, blood-curdling scream that was fully audible above the cacophony of the conveyor belts. A whistle was blowing, as it did when there was an accident, and a woman's voice was still screaming and shouting above the din. All the conveyor belts ground to a shuddering halt and the women had an unexpected break.

'What is it?' whispered Betty to Ena, who had a better view, down the side aisle.

'It's Lil,' said Ena. 'You know, in collars. An accident, looks like.'

A maintenance man in blue overalls appeared, half-running, followed by someone in a suit from the office. 'Might as well tek a break,' whispered Ena, always practical, and they both slipped off their stools and stretched. As she did, Betty felt as if a giant hand had got hold of her baby bump and squeezed it.

'Oh!' she shouted out, involuntarily.

'What's up?' said Ena.

Betty held either side of her bump, feeling pale and afraid. 'Ah, don't know …'

The squeeze came again and knocked the breath out of her.

'Go and sit down,' said Ena, taking her arm. 'Come on, let's go outside to the lavvy.'

They went outside to the ladies' tiny, smelly lavatory. It was full of women taking advantage of poor Lil's accident to have an illicit ciggie, so it was full of smoke.

'D'yer need to go?' asked Ena.

Betty's eyes were like saucers. 'Ah don't know, ah feel funny.'

Ena looked at her face carefully. 'Nothing dribbling down yer leg yet?'

Betty looked at Ena, confused. 'No, why?'

Ena rolled her eyes and leaned in. 'Don't yer know,

when yer due, yer water's break. Ah've had three, ah should know …' She laughed raucously.

No, Betty didn't know. She was blissfully ignorant about what was going to happen. She vaguely understood that the baby had to come out the way it went in, but apart from that the details of the mechanics were a mystery to her. She just assumed her mother would help her with it all when she got there.

Ena lit two cigarettes and handed one to Betty, who drew on it hard as they moved along the toilet queue. 'Yer'll be all right, it's just the shock probably,' said Ena.

Betty had another strong abdominal squeeze, but by the time she got to the toilet she was feeling a bit more stable. Ena and Betty made their way back to their workstations, five minutes later.

'Yer took yer time,' snapped Mrs Dunn, who was waiting for them.

'Ah didn't feel well—' started Betty.

''Eck as like. Yer took advantage of Lil sewing up 'er 'and. Next time yer ask permission.' And with that, she stomped off, back over to Lil's workstation.

'False alarm,' whispered Ena. 'Yer get these cramps as yer get near yer time, it's perfectly normal.'

With that, the conveyor belt jumped into life and the women got back to their daily grind.

*

Of course, when the baby eventually came, it was not only late but it came in the middle of the night.

Betty, now twenty-three, had always been an anxious young woman, and worried intensely that the baby was overdue. Was it all right? Was there anything she could or should do? Her mother told her it was fine, but, when she went two weeks beyond her due date, she began to get really worried.

'Our Dorothy was late, babies often are, so I wouldn't fret,' reassured Sophia.

All her baby clothes were now knitted, folded and neatly piled up, ready for use. They had bought a dozen terrycloth nappies and some Dettol and Woolite Laundry Soak to disinfect and clean them in a bucket after use. Sophia had even knitted a little teddy bear, which sat waiting in the basket weave carrycot she had used for all her own children and had now passed on to Betty.

Betty had carried on at work, but as her time drew near it was harder than ever to get up and down off the stool.

'Yer need a crane,' joked Ena, making Betty laugh. 'Sure it's not twins?'

However, the baby was coming now, as her waters had broken in a cascade down her legs, just as Ena had said they would. Betty had been in labour for about four hours, walking up and down the bedroom, puffing and blowing. It was agony.

Arthur went out and phoned the midwife from the phone box and at about five in the morning the midwife appeared carrying her bag of tricks. She examined Betty and said the baby was coming, but it would be a while yet. Arthur had to go to work, as normal, and the midwife said she would be back later. Betty felt terrified to be alone, but eventually at seven the midwife came back and she was examined again.

'Hmmm,' said the midwife, feeling Betty's tummy, and examining her internally. She then said, ponderously. 'Ah'm not sure if baby is breach. Ah think ah'd like doctor to tek a look at yer. Reckon we should get you to the General.'

In the hospital Betty was still waiting. It was now ten hours since her waters had broken. She desperately wanted her mother to come, but she was still working as a cleaner, plus hospitals were very strict at the time and visiting was only allowed at specific times, an hour in the afternoon between 3 and 4pm, and in the evening, from 7.30 to 8.30. So Betty had to wait and endure alone.

Eventually, the baby was born via forceps with some difficulty and a lot of gas and air. Betty was on her own with a doctor and a nurse, and the baby was wrapped up and taken away to be weighed. She was exhausted. Betty then delivered the placenta, which was something she had not expected. Finally, she had to be stitched up by the doctor, as she had a tear from the forceps delivery, and the doctor did it without anaesthetic, which was painful. Betty had never known anything like the agony or the physical exhaustion, and it was as if her body had been through a giant mincer. However, it was all over now, and the baby was born.

Betty waited and waited for what seemed like hours. She was calm at first, but became increasingly alarmed when the nurse did not bring her baby back. Betty drifted off into sleep in a cloud of exhaustion, only to wake suddenly and wonder where her baby was. What had happened to it? Where was it? Why was everything so mysterious? Betty felt panic rising. What was going on? Her breasts were now hard as footballs and hurting badly, and she didn't understand why. Yet, her bed was clean, her sheets had been changed, as had her nightdress – this must have happened while she slept. But still there was no baby.

Eventually, the staff nurse came along and stood at the end of the bed. 'I'm sorry, but the baby was stillborn.'

Betty was unable to understand. She looked at the staff nurse, unable to take in what she was saying. Her body filled with ice, her blood slowed. 'What do you mean, stillborn?'

'I'm sorry,' said the staff nurse, awkwardly. 'There was nothing we could do. Is your husband coming in?'

Betty couldn't speak, she couldn't move, she couldn't think. Her body felt battered and her mind felt numb.

When she saw Arthur coming up the hospital ward towards her with a bunch of home-grown anemones in his hand, the tears began to flow.

'Oh, Arthur,' sighed Betty. 'Oh, no. Oh no, no, no ...' and she began to sob her heart out.

Arthur was confused, shocked, then devastated. He put his arm around Betty and held her as she mourned the loss her lovely baby, their baby. When the staff nurse came back to check Betty's temperature with a glass thermometer, Arthur tried to get some more information, but she was impervious.

'I'm sorry,' said the staff nurse somewhat starchily, 'The baby was not viable, it didn't survive.'

Arthur could not understand. Was it a girl? Was it a boy? Was something wrong, like a disease? Or a deformity?

'I'm sorry,' repeated the staff nurse, 'That's all I can tell you.'

Indeed, Arthur and Betty never saw their baby. They never said goodbye. They had no idea what happened to it or why it had died. They didn't christen it. There wasn't a funeral. It just disappeared. It remained an 'it'. They never knew whether 'it' was a boy or a girl.

The only reminder it ever existed was Betty's breasts, which were overflowing with milk for a baby that wasn't there, and it was the worst thing in the world. She was given something to dry up the milk, which upset her even more. Women on the ward, all around her, were feeding their babies and she could hear babies crying all the time. It was torture. Were they punishing her?

Luckily, Sophia arrived before the end of visiting time, and taking one look at Betty and Arthur's tragic faces and empty arms, she knew instantly. She burst into tears, and they sat, all three, in mournful silence. There was nothing to say. Sophia had a hundred questions, but she could see her daughter was beyond talking.

'Visiting Hour is over,' said the staff nurse, ringing a little brass bell, and Sophia and Arthur had to go, leaving Betty to face her childless night alone.

Betty's baby was dead, her baby was not coming home; their baby was not alive, had disappeared, but poor Betty still couldn't really take it in. The baby she had spent months feeling in her tummy, that had whirled around when she was at work and jumped in her abdomen, and 'quickened' when she was in bed at night. She would never meet that child, or get to see their little fingers and toes, and look into their tiny blue eyes. The baby would never wear its little hats and mittens or the jackets that she had made.

That night in Nottingham General was the worst night that Betty could ever remember. Worse than her father dying, worse than Arnold dying. She had had so much to look forward to with her own beloved Arthur. She had worked for nine months imagining the life they would now live together, the three of them in their little house on Cambria Street. Now all of that had been snatched away. There was no baby. Her baby was dead. Gone. She was utterly and completely heartbroken.

Betty rolled over and sobbed out her heart and felt it was the absolute end of the world.

8

A long Life of Toil

All her working life Betty was a machinist in Nottingham's 'dark satanic mills'. She toiled for thirty-six long years doing the same or similar job, day in, day out, uncomplaining and hard-working.

After the tragic and unexplained death of her child, she went to work in Arnold, a suburb of Nottingham, in a Sybille Claymore factory. She began to make whole blouses for the fashion industry, but was still at her machine all day. She felt limited in her career choices as her poor schooling had drummed into her that she was not good with words, but Betty was always conscientious and diligent, and earned her way through thick and thin.

Betty was heartbroken when her beloved husband Arthur died. However, a few years later she met another Arthur who worked at Boots and they married. Too late for children, they settled into a happy life together. Betty continued working until she retired at sixty. Betty and her new husband travelled to New Zealand to visit her brother, Morris, who had emigrated there. They also had other great foreign holidays.

Then Arthur died, sadly. Like her mother before her, Betty outlived two husbands. Added to this was the tender, eternal pain of losing her child, which cast a long shadow over her life, although she was not bitter.

Betty threw herself into maintaining her garden beautifully, going to church and into being a doting aunt to her sister Dorothy's children, grandchildren and great-grandchildren. She turned ninety in the summer of 2016 and is still going strong.

Albert Godfrey

Albert on the RMS *Queen Mary*.

Tim

CORINNE SWEET

for flowers, vegetables and fruit

in the Meadows, and the are

Of course, the decla

had meant everythi

whole family ha

hole in the

Anderso

The

In the suburl
Meadows, fi
for his father to
Godfrey senior
– Shipstones –
labourer. It wa ... time Nottingham
boasted three major breweries – Shipstones, Home
Brewery and Kimberley Ales – all providing beer to
hundreds of pubs and thousands of workers. Beer was the
daily emollient for all ills; physical, social and spiritual.
Pre-television, pubs, like churches, were the lifeblood of
the community.

The Godfreys, Albert and Mabel, and sons Ernest
and little Albert, had originally started out their life in
a run-down red-brick terrace, very similar to Betty's in
Traffic Street in the Meadows, but had been moved out
when the slum clearance began and the bulldozers moved
in. Now the family felt lucky to live in a relatively new
semi-detached council house that had been built in the
1920s – still rented but with a bit of garden out the back

The air was fresher than
                              a didn't flood as often.
                         ...tion of war in September 1939
                    ...g changed, and in preparation the
                   ...d rolled up their sleeves and dug a deep
              ...back garden for their government-issued
          ...n shelter, which they also constructed themselves.
         ...windows of the semi now had blackout curtains and
...hey had strengthened the glass against bomb blasts by
taping a white X on each pane. There were sandbags
stacked out back, just in case. The family had become
used to ducking into the shelter any time night or day
when the wailing air-raid sirens screamed their warnings
and the German bombers came. Plus they had to carry
their smelly black rubber gas masks in their khaki canvas
shoulder bags everywhere they went.

Every night, despite the war, Albert junior liked to
look down Quarry Road to see his father heave into
view in his black donkey jacket, worsted flat cap and
brown workman's boots. His father would come into
the kitchen, saying 'Ayup' to everyone and no one, then
fling his jacket and cap on the hook on the door. Young
Albert loved the strong yeasty smell of the brewery that
came in with his father, but he didn't go up and hug
him as he was usually both dirty and grumpy in equal
measure. Albert would watch as his father went straight
to the kitchen sink, rolled up his sleeves and washed his

hands and face thoroughly with Pears' soap and a bristle nail brush. The blue-and-white striped towel would be black once he'd done.

That night, Albert's mother carried on cooking, hardly acknowledging her husband when he came in, despite his proximity. She was standing at the gas stove in her flowery apron, stirring the contents of a large aluminium saucepan with a big wooden spoon while poking the potatoes boiling in another saucepan with a knife to see if they were done.

'Go and get me some mint, will yer?' she called over to little Albert, who went out the back door and down the step to pluck some fresh green leaves from a little terracotta pot. He ran back in with his little verdant fistful, excited by completing his mission and hopefully pleasing his mother, who took the mint leaves and threw them into the boiling potatoes. 'Tea's up,' she snapped.

Ernest, Albert's thirteen-year-old brother, who attended the local grammar school, was still wearing his uniform of a smart navy blazer and grey shorts. He was deep in his schoolbooks as usual, writing with an air of concentration at the kitchen table, oblivious of everything.

'I said, "tea's up" Ernest, d'yer hear? Can yer move thyssen …?'

At his mother's stern tone, Ernest's head rose from his homework. As she came towards the table with a steaming pot in both her hands, he swept his books into his battered black briefcase.

'Albert, lay't table, will yer?'

Little Albert went to the front drawer of the walnut veneer sideboard, reached up and got out four raffia mats and a knife and fork for everyone, while Mabel put down two bread boards and plonked the stew and the potatoes in their steaming saucepans on each of them.

Mabel dished out the lamb and vegetable hotpot for the third day running. It was padded out with potatoes, as it was getting pretty thin now. There was hardly any meat to be had, just carrots and turnips, and Mabel made sure the biggest bits of meat ended up on Albert senior's plate. Then came Ernest, then Albert, and on hers there was just a bit of sauce, carrots and potatoes. Mother and Father weren't speaking, little Albert noticed, and he had that cramped, tight feeling in his tummy that he often had these days. There always seemed to be something to feel worried about, and he didn't like how he felt when they all sat down at the table to eat. The atmosphere was as unsavoury as the hotpot on his plate, so Albert kept his head down and cleaned up his food in record time.

Albert senior opened a bottle of Shippos Extra Stout with a metal opener, then he poured it into a stumpy glass, admiring the thick, frothy head that formed on the top. As he took a big gulp, Mabel watched him like a hawk, then crossed her arms.

'It won't do, Albert.' She looked fiercely at the beer, then up at his face, peeved.

Albert senior examined the froth on his beer and took another big gulp.

'We need more money,' Mabel said pointedly.

Albert junior stared first at his mother, then at his father, then at his empty plate. This was an uncomfortably familiar scene that played out regularly at home. Ernest kept his eyes on his own plate, while Albert senior speared another potato with his fork and put it in his mouth whole, chewing intently.

'Ah can't manage on what yer bring home from't brewery.' Still no response. 'Ah think … Ah think ah should get me'self a job.'

At this Albert came to life. He pushed away his plate with a clatter and threw himself back on his chair at an angle, looking Mabel straight in the eye for the first time that evening. He crossed his arms, mirroring her stance. 'Yer what?'

Both little Albert and Ernest knew what usually happened at this point and it wasn't fun. Ernest picked up his plate and quietly slunk away from the table, putting it carefully in the sink. He picked up his heavy briefcase and tiptoed out of the kitchen door, clearly hoping not to be seen. Little Albert, however, was nailed to the spot as the drama unfolded along horribly familiar lines, like a train running on a well-worn track.

'No wife of mine is going to work,' said Albert senior, forcefully.

'But Albert ...' implored Mabel.

'No "buts". Ah won't 'ave it,' interjected Father. 'Ah won't an' that's that. I work long hours at Shippos, not for nowt, either.'

In answer, Mother collected up the plates noisily and clattered them onto the drainer by the window that overlooked the back garden with its arched corrugated-iron Anderson shelter at the bottom. Little Albert was scared and didn't know whether he should get down, like Ernest, or stay at the table. He started fidgeting, watching Mother put in the plug and start running water into the sink. Her back seemed to speak volumes, but he didn't know what it said.

Albert senior, meanwhile, let his chair fall back with a heavy 'thunk' and took a final swig of his stout, smacked his lips, polishing it off with satisfaction. He rested his muscular arms along the table and sighed, watching his wife's reproachful back while she washed and slammed plate after plate into the suspended wooden plate rack on the wall.

'Angela works,' she said sulkily to the plates. 'So does Doris ... Where's the 'arm – everyone's doing their bit.'

That was it. Father's fuse was lit. 'Fer heaven's sake, woman, can you stop yer bleddy cracked record! It's hard enough fer us men to find work right now, even with a war on, so why should they give a job to you? Stop yer bellyaching.'

Albert's father was aggrieved that he had to work instead of signing up. He'd served his King and Country in the final year of the Great War, and had been injured and demobbed as 'unfit' to fight. The Depression had hit him hard and he'd had a tough time being unemployed, as many ex-soldiers did. Even with his injuries he could still work as a manual labourer, and Shipstones offered regular if low-paid work, hefting crates, unloading drays, rolling kegs, making deliveries to local pubs with a horse and cart, sweeping the floor and being the general dogsbody. So at home he needed to feel he was king of the castle, and no wife of his was going to show him up by going out to work. He wanted, *needed*, to be the main provider.

Furious, Albert senior got to his feet, grabbed his discarded black jacket and cap off the door hook and slammed out of the front door.

Off to the Beehive, thought little Albert. It was his father's favourite pub. Inside he was trembling, feeling hollow and cold. His mother continued to wash up, and Albert sat at the table not knowing what to do, his little heart pumping away.

The kitchen door opened and Ernest crept back in and plonked his briefcase back down at the table, and Albert started breathing again. Mother finished the washing up in hurt silence and took her pinny off, hanging it carefully over the back of a kitchen chair.

In Albert's mind a simple message had taken root: money was important, there was never enough of it, and grown-ups were always shouting about it for some unknown reason. Money mattered a lot. Albert thought, in his childlike way, he'd have to go and get a job as soon as he was big enough. He wanted to make his mother happy, so he'd soon have to be a real man, going out to work, like Father, otherwise there'd never be enough to go round.

Clearly, there was a war going on both inside and outside the house.

2
Trainee Dogsbody

'Ah'm goin' down't pit,' said Benji. He looked pleased with himself. 'Gedling, like me ol' man.'

Benji was sitting nestled into the top V of a huge oak tree's giant spreading branches in Sherwood Forest, which backed on to Bulwell village. Albert, now thirteen, looked at Benji's ruddy face and dishevelled hair, at his scabby knees, filthy rumpled socks and scuffed shoes and thought, T'pit's not for me.

'Well, ah'm off ter Players, they pay better'n Boots, that's fer sure,' said Ted, lying along a branch lower down. 'Me grandad's at t' factory and says it's grand. Free ciggies an' all.'

The boys laughed. Ted was red in the face from running, as they'd been kicking an old leather football about in the woods for an hour. 'An' Grandad says they still 'av' tunnels underneath from t'war,' Ted finished off proudly.

'Crikey!' said Benji. 'Get away wi' yer,' and he nearly fell off his branch taking an enthusiastic swipe with his foot at Ted's head.

'Tis true,' retorted Ted. 'Five thousand workers 'id down there at a time – to stop the bleddy Germans.'

Albert was only listening vaguely to the chatter overhead. He was lying under the tree on the cool grass beneath his friends with a half-drunk bottle of fizzy dandelion and burdock in hand. He watched the sun twinkle through the branches; he loved to watch it flashing in and out of the mass of white and green fronds. Ted mentioning the war brought to his mind the major Blitz in Nottingham when he was about five years old, when almost two hundred people had died and many more were injured. He remembered seeing churches and buildings demolished, with rubble everywhere, and people crying and shaking their heads. He heard his parents talking mournfully about the old Co-op Bakery in Meadow Lane being hit and all the workers killed. He could still see in his mind's eye the shocking black-and-white pictures in the paper. There were still bombed-out areas to explore, not only in the city, just a bus ride away, but in their own village.

'What about yer, Albert?' shouted Benji from his prime lookout position up the tree. 'Whatcher goin' ter do?'

'Ah dunno yet,' said Albert, pensively. ''Aven't decided.'

The end of school was rapidly coming towards them all and Albert was under pressure to decide what to do. His mother still moaned constantly about money and his father still worked at Shippos. Albert loved being outdoors with his friends. Benji, Ted and he had enjoyed their years in Bulwell, not only at the infants school but also at the secondary modern, where they were all average students. They were also in the local Scouts and loved football. Most Sundays, Albert went to the Methodist church with his mother, sang in the choir and spent time with the youth group. He liked rambling and camping, sometimes going into Derbyshire to walk the hills and dales, despite the uncertainty of the war years.

Most of Albert's friends were going the way of Benji and Ted: working at the six local pits (which paid the best), Players, the Raleigh (as it was fondly known locally) or Boots. But Albert wanted to do something different. He imagined himself sitting on a high stool, smartly dressed in a dark suit and crisp white shirt, writing neatly with a pen and ink in a heavy leather-bound ledger. Although he was not top at school, certainly not a high achiever like Ernest, who, much to his parents' pride, was now training as an accountant, Albert liked the idea of a clean office job. But he was hardly going to tell his friends that as he was bound to get a ribbing.

'Albert Godfrey?' Albert looked across the desk at the fierce middle-aged woman sitting opposite him. She wore a woolly blue suit, her hair was tightly permed, and tortoiseshell glasses were perched on the end of her nose. 'Why do you want the job?'

'I ... er ...' Albert shuffled on the hard wooden seat, and swallowed hard. 'Well, er ... I ... er ... saw the advert in't paper and thought it looked interesting.'

'Hmmm ...' The woman, who had introduced herself as Mrs Tierney, scrutinised Albert's application form and then looked at Albert as if she was appraising a piece of pork at the butcher's. She took in his clean shirt, scrubbed appearance and slicked-down black hair. Albert looked smart enough and had clearly made an effort. He was personable, quite handsome and well turned out, if a bit shy. 'Do you know anything about the law?' she snipped.

Albert gulped and could feel his heart racing. This was harder that he had realised. 'Er, no, not really ...' said Albert, honestly. 'But ahm willing to learn.'

Mrs Tierney looked at her watch, 'Well ... we are very busy here,' she said officiously, 'so I might as well show you the ropes.'

She stood up and indicated that Albert should follow. They were in Browne and Jacobson's, a lawyer's firm in Friar's Lane near Wheelergate in central Nottingham. There was bomb damage in the road which Albert had taken a look at on the way with interest. It fascinated him to see the insides of buildings, with their wallpaper and sinks exposed to air and filling with wild plants. Today, he was excited, if somewhat awed, to be in a proper business building, with real lawyers doing important things. Spread over three floors and made in the red-brick, late-Gothic Victorian style, the lawyers' offices looked imposing from the outside. Inside, they seemed to go on for ever.

Mrs Tierney was still talking. 'And here is the post room. This is where you'll pick up letters and parcels and deliver them round to the secretaries …'

When they ended up back at the front reception lobby Mrs Tierney said, 'So I'll see you Monday morning, nine sharp,' and it was only then that Albert realised he'd been hired. He had got his first job. Albert floated down the road, elated by his success. He was all of fourteen and on his way in life.

On his first proper day of work, father and son sat on the bus into Nottingham in comfortable silence. Albert was wearing his best and only dark brown Sunday suit, which was a bit short in the leg, with double turn-ups and braces. Both father and son sported grey worsted caps, as most men did at the time. Albert senior got off first to change buses, and patted his son on the back, 'Good luck, lad,' which warmed Albert junior's heart.

Once in the office, Mrs Tierney took Albert round, but it was hard for him to take it all in. On the second floor, there was a long room full of wooden desks in rows with black typewriters on them and smartly dressed women – who didn't even look up as he passed – clacking away at high speed. This was what Mrs Tierney called 'the typing pool'. Then they passed down endless corridors lined with a few impressive-looking offices that had wooden doors with gold lettering on the glass windows.

'You'll be making the tea here, in the service kitchen,' explained Mrs Tierney brusquely, as she showed him the room, 'then taking it round the staff.'

Albert was horrified as he had never mashed tea before, especially in such a huge pot. He looked at the neat green cups and saucers that were so very different from the thick white mugs at home. There was a box of tempting Huntley and Palmers biscuits and he had to put these on a plate ('No filching, mind,' said Mrs Tierney darkly), along with a green bowl filled with sugar cubes and silver tongs. Mrs Tierney showed him how many tablespoons of loose tea to put in the pot, and how to stir it first before pouring it out through a huge tea-strainer. She also taught him how to lift the sugar lumps into the cups with the tongs. There was a rattling metal hostess trolley he had to push around the floors, going up and down in a service lift, which Albert found fun.

As well as the tea ceremony, which took place twice a day, Albert also had to distribute the post round the main secretaries, who were unnervingly pretty women, but who didn't even look up at him when he arrived, lugging his heavy canvas sack. However, there was a really enjoyable part of the job, which involved going outside. He would be sent out to deliver official 'bundles' of lawyers' papers tied in pink ribbon and he'd run down the bustling Nottingham streets to local solicitors' offices, or even to the grand county court on Maid Marion Way.

'Ah, the new lad,' said Mr Goldstein, as Albert knocked tentatively on the accountant and bookkeeper's door. The second desk in the room was occupied by Mrs Brayburn who, with her tight grey bun and grey suit, blended into the grey filing cabinets that lined the room. Albert stood in front of Mr Goldstein's desk, which was heaped with manila folders, a dark-green desk lamp and an overflowing ashtray. Mr Goldstein opened a desk drawer and rummaged for a moment, and then produced a little brown envelope. 'Your first wages, lad. Better count it.'

Albert took the package gingerly and opened it. It was real money. Notes and coins: £1.6s.3d. Money at last.

As Albert pocketed the cash, Mr Goldstein went back to his books while Mrs Brayburn got up, opened a huge creaking drawer and filed some papers. Albert noticed an enormous ledger with rows and rows of figures in neat black ink and, upside down, he could see his name at the bottom, with a tick beside it.

'That's all,' snapped Mr Goldstein, waving Albert away with his hand, 'Be on time next Monday. There's many more where you came from.' And with that, Albert was dismissed.

Back in Bulwell, walking up Quarry Street, Albert felt a huge surge of pride. His first pay packet. He'd earned it all himself. His heart nearly burst out of his chest as he placed the money on the kitchen table in front of his mother. She picked it up, and smiled briefly, but then said, 'It's not a lot, but it'll do.'

Albert's joy was dented by his mother's words – he'd obviously need to get a better paying job.

3

Moving On

Early, one crisp September morning in 1951, fifteen-year-old Albert whistled to himself as he walked briskly along Traffic Street in the Meadows towards his new job at Furse Wholesale Ltd, having left Browne and Jacobson, the legal firm, just the week before. It was a peerless day with bright sunshine, even though there was already an autumnal bite in the air. It is just possible Albert might have spied a bob of curly blond hair belonging to Betty, as she rushed to her shirt-machining job at the other end of Traffic Street, at Cellular Clothing, where she still worked.

Albert felt really optimistic as he joined the throng of workers going in the tradesman's entrance, as he had upped his pay by a few shillings (which pleased his mother) and felt this was a step up from the solicitors' office. Most local people said, 'You can walk out of a job on Monday and go and get another one on Tuesday; leave that, and you'll get another one on Wednesday,' and Albert discovered it was true, especially in low-paid work, where there was a great deal of ebb and flow of the workforce.

Furse Wholesale was an enormous company that dealt in electrical goods and installation. Their Nottingham branch also built lifts and theatrical equipment, so there were vast warehouses out the back. Albert had imagined he would be dealing with customers, as the advert had talked about 'sales' in the paper, and at the interview he'd been told the job was going to entail selling, rather than just tea-making and delivering the post. However, he was somewhat disappointed to find himself back in the post room on day one, doing very menial jobs all over again.

'Ayup,' said Mr Fraser, the head of the post room, as Albert arrived from the tradesmen's entrance, where he'd been shown to clock in. Mr Fraser was standing by the wooden letterboxes with staff name labels painted on them, which covered a whole wall, floor to ceiling. He was dressed in brown workman's overalls, which seemed to be a Furse uniform, at least for the manual staff. He also had on big black boots and was drawing hard on a cigarette. 'Can yer sort t' post,' he said to Albert, exhaling a stream of smoke. He pointed to about six hessian sacks of post which had come in that morning.

'Yes, sir,' said Albert, and he started picking out letters and matching them to the A to Z of staff names. The job was fun, at first, but it meant he had to get a stepladder to climb up to the top pigeon-holes a dozen times, and after a while his legs were really aching. Eventually the job was done, and Albert stood back, satisfied. He went to find Mr Fraser, who was sat at a wooden desk, covered with envelopes and sticky tape and all sorts.

'Ahm done, sir,' said Albert politely.

Mr Fraser looked up slowly from his paperwork and stood up. 'Foller me, lad.'

Dutifully, Albert followed him back out to the postal area where he'd been working. He hadn't noticed the ten sacks stuffed with post and packages that were ready to go in the corner of the room. 'Can yer frank this little lot?' he said to Albert, pointing to the parcels.

'Yes, sir,' said Albert, and rolled up his sleeves.

Mr Fraser showed him how to weigh and stamp the packages, and then Albert spent the next couple of hours tightening their strings, checking their labels and stuffing them into enormous hessian GPO sacks.

'Right lad, can yer go t'warehouse and fetch us thirty boxes,' asked Mr Fraser when Albert reported back to him that he had finished. 'Use the platform trolley.'

So off Albert trotted, down several staircases and out the back to a huge yard with carts and trucks, and he picked up what he hoped was a platform trolley and went and found some boxes in one of the warehouses for Mr Fraser, whistling to himself all the while. He suddenly heard someone cat-calling across the yard and could see a couple of lads making faces and gesturing at him. Albert knew better than to engage and just nodded at them, looking neutral. He didn't want any trouble; he wanted this job.

Albert's first couple of weeks were spent fetching and carrying stationery and boxes, or franking packages and letters, or taking out rubbish to the big metal waste bins, sweeping the floor, putting toilet rolls in the lavatories, making up boxes of electrical goods for posting or delivery and making tea in a giant aluminium teapot, yet again, for staff over several floors. At least he knew how to do that now. There were no sugar tongs here, just a sticky teaspoon and a bag of white granulated Tate and Lyle sugar. Whatever the most menial tasks were, Albert did them.

After a while, he began to get a bit fed up: nobody was talking to him, he felt like he didn't really exist, and he had no sort of real job to do. It was all too repetitive – he'd wanted something he could really get his teeth into. In fact, he just felt like a glorified donkey. He had a fantasy (after the one about writing in a ledger with pen and ink had been dispelled at the solicitors) of meeting people face to face and selling them things. He was a sociable young man and liked chatting to his friends at church or on a walk in the forest, or kicking a ball with his old schoolmates. He missed that kind of human interaction in his menial workplace dungeon. He'd begun to like the idea of sales, and imagined himself in a suit, like the lawyers had worn, as he liked dressing smartly.

It would make him feel good about himself, like he was going up in the world.

One dinnertime, he screwed up all his courage up and approached his supervisor, Mr Fraser, the avuncular man who had trained him up from the beginning. Albert felt his palms sweating and his heart pumping, but he had an important question to ask him. 'Ahem ... excuse me, Mr Fraser,' said Albert.

Mr Fraser was biting into a crusty cheese cob with the *Nottingham Evening Post* on his lap open at the racing pages. He looked up at Albert, who felt embarrassed, but knew he had to ask. 'Mr Fraser, sir, can ah ... can ah ... do summat more, well, interesting?'

Mr Fraser cocked his head to one side and kept chewing.

'Ah mean,' continued Albert, 'ah'd hoped to do summat more like selling ... y'know, selling electrical goods and such.'

Mr Fraser swallowed. 'Oh, ah see,' he said. 'Feel it's a bit beneath yer, eh?' He was teasing. Or was it testing?

'Yes,' said Albert quickly. 'Well, no,' he panicked. 'Oh, dear ...' He didn't know quite what to say.

Mr Fraser looked bemused and finished his roll. Albert knew he didn't want to be a general labourer like his dad. He'd seen the strife it caused at home. Albert wanted something more, something better, something more creative, more engaging and, of course, something which paid better. His mother still wanted him to earn more … and he did, as well.

Mr Fraser watched him closely for a moment, 'Y'know we all 'ave to start somewhere,' he said, pointedly. Albert was crestfallen. 'But ah'll 'ave a word – you're a good lad.'

Albert beamed.

4

Gift of the Gab

Six months later, Albert was walking down a street in Houndsgate to Lace Market in central Nottingham. He passed bombed-out buildings with weeds growing in their debris. It was a reminder that the war was only just over, and Nottingham was still trying hard to get itself back on its feet. He was now in the retail and business hub of the city and he stopped in front of an expansive gothic building which had Richard Lunt & Co in gold lettering sprawled across the front.

Before he hopped up the steps, Albert, wearing his brown double-breasted suit, polished his shoes on the back of his trousers, straightened his tie and slicked down his hair with his hands. His previous job at Furse's had not developed further – despite Mr Fraser's promises, he'd continued to be the donkey dogsbody. Albert felt the burning beat of ambition in his soul. Eventually, he had been put on a tradesman's desk, selling wires and cables and other electrical goods to electricians, but it wasn't a job that fired up his imagination.

One evening at home, he had seen an advert for a 'trainee gentleman salesman' in the classifieds section of the *Post*, and he'd leapt at it, writing a letter that evening. Everyone knew Richard Lunt's, even though it was only one of ten enormous textile companies in the Lace Market area. The textile business had begun to pick up, post-war, as everyone was getting interested in having new clothes and starting life afresh. Richard Lunt was a prestigious firm, and Albert believed the job had promise. After a short interview, with a severe, yet appropriately named Mrs Draper, Albert was offered a job and entered a fascinating emporium that was spread across several floors: haberdashery, knitting wools, menswear, ladies' wear, boots and shoes, outerwear, and even underwear (including fancy ladies' lingerie). Richard Lunt's was a wholesaler to the retail trade, so although the company was not selling directly to the public, Albert would be working with people face to face.

Mr Davidson, a very dapper man in a black suit, who looked a bit like the popular actor Dennis Price, was to train Albert in the art of selling. 'You have to be very polite,' explained Mr Davidson, to a willing but tense Albert. 'We get in new stock all the time and the buyers want to know what is coming into fashion next season. They like to be ahead of their competitors.' Albert took note. 'You need to show them the range of colours and try and secure a multiple sale of each item. You can let them take it on a "sale or return basis".'

Albert's eyes widened, 'What's that?'

Mr Davidson cleared his throat, with a slightly superior air. 'It means the buyers take, say, five or even thirty of one style of coat, in several colours, and you write out a chit for them. If they don't sell them all within sixty days, they can return them for new or different stock.' Also there was a system, Mr Davidson said, 'Where the buyers can take a garment on "appro" and that means they take it, and if they don't bring it back within ten days, they'll be charged for it.'

'What's "appro"?' asked Albert, innocently.

'Approval, of course,' snapped Mr Davidson rolling his eyes heavenward.

He also explained the buyers might come and look at the merchandise, then go back and ring up or write a formal letter to make an order. In which case, it was up to Albert to issue a 'Bill of Lading' that went out with the clothing when it was despatched.

'You need to keep abreast of fashion,' Mr Davidson said with a sniff. 'See what colours are popular. You know the ladies like their skirts full now, and men are still double-breasted in suits, but you need to understand what they need for every occasion. Plus you'll need to think about accessories – gloves, scarves, hats and the like.'

Albert saw instantly he would have a job on his hands to find out what people were wearing, what was fashionable and understand what sold well. Albert loved going to the cinema when he could, read the paper regularly and liked to keep up with things, so he knew he would have to do some research. However, he really wanted to do as well as Benji and Ted. His friends down the pit and at the Raleigh and even Players, were still earning better than he was. When they met in the park, or at a social, in Bulwell, it was still a sore point when they compared their hourly rates as they kicked a ball about. Albert knew he needed to pay attention to improve his earnings.

'Do your homework,' Mr Davidson said finally. 'Get your order book full to the brim.'

'Yes, sir,' said Albert, his heart racing. 'Right away.'

In fact, it took Albert several months to get into the swing of selling. It was a complicated job and he had a lot to learn. The buyers were always in a hurry, and nearly always knew what they wanted (or thought they did). They were also very choosy, and fussy about detail, and some people were very rude. Albert learned he had to approach them respectfully, but with a warm and open demeanour. He liked to engage them in conversation, asking, 'How was your journey, sir?' or 'Nice weather we're having, madam' to warm them up. However, sometimes a buyer would come in and snap, 'Show us what yer've got – ah haven't time to waste, son.' Even so, Albert took pride in showing them the latest raglan sleeve button-through cable cardigan, in four pastel shades, or the newest camel swing coat or satinised cotton duster coat. Albert was learning to sell to small local shops, to buyers who went back to their shops in surrounding villages, and, finally, to the big department stores in central Nottingham, like Jessops on Long Row, Griffin and Spalding (which eventually became Debenhams), and Pearsons. He also learned to be interested in people as they came to buy, and developed relationships with the buyers to get their return business.

In the post-war world, money was tight, but Albert knew that people wanted desperately to wear something new, something colourful, something fresh and different, after the drab and restrictive war years. Women were fed up with their 'utility' clothing from the war and were snapping up spotty or floral dresses with cinched-in waists and full, circular skirts, and were even beginning to wear capri pants (trousers were not really worn much by women for leisure until then) and (not too short) shorts. After all the austerity, the emphasis was on fun and femininity.

Both men and women wore hats all the time, and there was a fantastic range of trilbies and bowlers, homburgs and caps, and for women close-fitting skullcaps with netting, or jaunty berets, or fancy millinery confections of every hue. Glamour was big, as Hollywood was

149

influencing cinemagoers, and women wanted to emulate Joan Crawford, Marilyn Monroe, Audrey Hepburn or Jayne Mansfield; men wanted to dress like Cary Grant, Joseph Cotton, Laurence Olivier or Alec Guinness.

Working for Richard Lunt's turned out to be an interesting job for Albert, as he was finding out about his own personality, and his strengths and his weaknesses. He settled into a new daily routine. He would have breakfast at home, made by his mother – toast and sometimes a boiled egg and tea. Then he'd hop on the number 43 or 54 bus, and get to the office by nine. This was more leisurely than factory workers who had to be in by seven or eight at the latest. For dinner, he'd take a cheese or an egg sandwich with him to save money and he took the opportunity to walk around Nottingham, wandering up to the castle to look at the views or strolling along to the Old Market Square. In the evenings, he went to the Methodist church youth club in Bulwell two or three times a week.

Characteristically, Albert decided to 'improve' himself further and enrolled at night school to learn shorthand and typing, which he did one night a week. He felt it strengthened his chances of more clerical work, which part of him still hankered after.

Money was still tight at home, as his father had not increased his meagre wage. In fact, he earned less than Albert, which Albert felt a little uncomfortable about sometimes. However, he was able to save for a summer holiday, which was a week of camping with the church youth club. During his first year at Richard Lunt's, he went to Mablethorpe in Lincolnshire, which was a popular seaside resort for workers in Nottingham. Albert felt very grown up to be able to pay for his own summer break.

Around this time, Albert started to want to go dancing. Most young people liked to go to the Victoria Ballroom, which was the local 'Palais de Danse'. Unlike most Nottinghamers, Albert didn't imbibe that much, he could have a drink one night, and leave it the next. He certainly didn't pack away the pints like his friends (and his father) who worked down the pits or on the factory floor. Partially, this was because of his religious belief. He was a 'fellow' of his church, and the fellowship he found there was an important and guiding part of his life. Seeing the damage done by his father's regular drinking and angry outbursts meant he felt he had to keep a check on himself, especially as he wanted to get on in the world. He linked drink to failure, and he certainly didn't want to fail, as he felt he definitely had more to learn and more of himself to give. What's more, he was keen to earn as much as he could to make his mother proud.

A couple of years later, and still working at Richard Lunt's, Albert was now established as a safe pair of selling hands. He managed a stint in the prestigious fur department, which paid more money as he was dealing with a luxury item usually reserved for wives of business-men or the wealthy few in Nottingham, and he enjoyed learning to tell his chinchilla from his mink, or his fox from his rabbit. Furs were very popular then, especially because of the Hollywood influence (Bette Davis or Barbara Stanwyck were always draped in fur, it was the ultimate symbol of glamour). Fur was, of course, well beyond the means of the ordinary working person, but it had become a symbol that you were a member of the rising middle class – a sign of having arrived or, at least, being on the way.

Albert had learned to cultivate his courteous and pleasant manner, and was becoming extremely good at closing a deal. One day, Mr Davidson watched Albert surreptitiously as he sold six full-length panelled, chestnut 'musquash' coats to a well-known dealer from Jessops, who was very hard to please. Albert had explained, 'These are the very latest fashion, very similar to Marilyn Monroe's garments. I am sure your clients will be clamouring for such an item this coming autumn.'

Afterwards, Mr Davidson bestowed on Albert his first proper badge of professional commendation. 'Well. You certainly have the gift of the gab, young man,' he said, almost warmly. 'Have you got any Irish in you, because you've certainly mastered the sales blarney?'

Albert laughed. Praise from Mr Davidson was rare praise indeed, and his jokes were almost non-existent. He realised then that he must have learned something about selling after all.

5

Gentleman's Outfitter

For two decades after his first job in retail sales at Richard Lunt's, Albert became an ace salesman. He moved from Richard Lunt's to a smaller, family firm, George H. Levy, who were in Wheeler Gate in Nottingham. The money was slightly better (which was always important), and Albert's experience was soon recognised and rewarded. However, the company sadly went bust. On the retail grapevine, Albert heard that the prestigious gentleman's outfitter Austin Reed was looking for staff. Albert applied, and found himself working in the 'crème de la crème' of men's retail.

Working for a company like Austin Reed was a completely new experience for Albert. It was a strict, traditional company, servicing the world of lawyers, judges, doctors, top executives and other members of the upper classes. Albert was taught that he should focus on helping the customer choose precisely what was right for him. His social skills were developed and put to the test under fierce scrutiny. It was a hierarchical company, with managers, under managers, assistant managers and many underlings, and Albert was to start at the bottom floor and work his way up. He had to wear a suit daily (by now he had two, a grey and a brown pinstripe), and some days he was allowed (even encouraged) to wear a tweed jacket, grey flannels and coloured tie, depending on what department he was in. On the ground floor were men's socks, pyjamas, ties, underwear and jewellery; on the next floor suits and shirts, and on the top floor, evening wear. There was a bonus scheme for sales, called a green ticket scheme. Albert could earn extra cash if he sold garments that had a green ticket, so he was highly motivated to up his selling game.

'When the customer arrives, you need to greet him politely,' explained Mr Marshall, a manager, shortly after Albert started work. Mr Marshall, a man in his late forties, was immaculately dressed in a dark lounge suit. 'You must identify, as quickly as possible, exactly what it is he is looking for, and then accommodate him.' Albert nodded, taking mental notes. 'You must ask if they are looking for anything in particular, and for what kind of occasion,' Mr Marshall paused for emphasis. 'Also ask them if they are looking for the same type of thing or if they wish to make a change ...'

Albert understood. He was taught to measure a gentleman with a white fabric tape measure, in a polite and discreet way, and to ask, with great delicacy, what he might be thinking of purchasing: 'Might I suggest a change, sir?' He soon understood that his customers were often particularly conservative, and thus had often ordered and re-ordered the same garments for years, just with bigger waistbands, and so Albert realised he had to be both creative and sensitive.

Albert worked in the shirt department for a while, which offered 365 different shirts, one for every day of the year, ranging from a small collar to a big collar, different sleeve lengths, colours and styles (probably made by the likes of Betty and her friends, down the road in Cellular Clothing). The manager in this department, Mr Higginbottom, was extremely strict and would run his fingers along the counters to check for dust and tut if anything was slightly unaligned. He would bark at Albert, 'Go down to the stock room and get yourself a dozen assorted pinstripes, size 16, and be quick about it.' Albert was taught: 'Never dawdle, or hang about the shop looking idle. Look alert, be smart, clean, well turned-out – we have to keep up standards.'

Albert had to be ready to serve even the most cantankerous of clients with charm and ease. He loved the job, finding it satisfying and prestigious. He liked the quiet, rarefied atmosphere and was proud that the firm felt itself to be the best in town. Although some customers were brusque or rude, he learned to remain calm and pleasant, even under pressure. He learned from Mr Marshall (and Mr Higginbottom), never to answer back, but to be constructive and diplomatic.

He was successful at the job, and began to gain good bonuses. 'Is Mr Godfrey in?' was a question Albert's colleagues heard a great deal. Albert was sought after as he gave such good personal treatment and attention to his clients. He seemed a favourite with the most crusty of old lawyers and judges, who could be very particular. They would wait until Albert came back from lunch, or finished with another customer, as they only wanted to be served by him.

One day Albert arrived at work, brushed his hair, checked his fingernails, straightened his tie, wiped away any crumbs from around his mouth and made his way to his floor. It was 1957, and he was working in the shirt department. Harold Macmillan had just become prime minister and the British public were being told that they'd 'never had it so good'. It was a new era, with mod cons like washing machines, fridges and even televisions beginning to arrive in people's homes. A sense of recovery after the grimness of the war years was in the air. Mr Marshall was waiting for Albert as he arrived in the shirt department, and stood at his section post. 'Come and see me at lunchtime, will you, Godfrey?'

'Yes, sir,' said Albert, almost saluting and clicking his heels.

At lunchtime (as he had now learned to call it, instead of dinner), Albert went and knocked on the glass window of Mr Marshall's tiny office in the back of the store. 'Ah, come in, Godfrey.'

Albert stood on the carpet, sweating into his suit, feeling very concerned. What had he done wrong? He racked his brains: he had made good sales the previous week, plenty of green tickets, too. Still, he knew to hold his tongue and wait for Mr Marshall to compose himself. 'I have been asked to put forward two men from this store by head office,' explained Mr Marshall, somewhat mysteriously. 'They want to know who are our best salesmen.' Albert still bit his tongue, waiting. 'So, I have suggested you, Godfrey.'

'Thank you, sir,' said Albert, somewhat relieved, but still not sure what all this was about.

Mr Marshall shuffled papers on his somewhat overcrowded desk and pulled out a manila folder. 'Ah, yes, here it is …' Albert swallowed. 'How would you like to man our shop on the *Queen Mary*?'

Albert's eyes nearly popped right out of his head. 'Excuse me, sir?'

'The *Queen Mary*,' Marshall said, shortly, 'The Cunard liner. We have a shop on her, and on the *Queen Elizabeth*. However, we need two staff for the *Queen Mary* to go to New York and back, in the autumn.' He paused as Albert took this in, his knees knocking together on the carpet, while staring at Mr Marshall in complete disbelief. 'Shall I put your name forward?'

Albert beamed a huge smile. 'Of course, sir, I mean, that would be absolutely wonderful. Yes, please, sir ...'

He didn't know what else to say. Images of his favourite film, *Singin' in the Rain*, floated through his mind, especially the 'Gotta Dance' scene when Gene Kelly hits the big city: yellow cabs, skyscrapers, the State of Liberty.

'That's all, back to your station, Godfrey,' said Mr Marshall, dismissively.

Albert floated out of the office and down the corridor, as if he were already crossing the Atlantic, in one of the most prestigious, glamorous vessels ever launched. The RMS *Queen Mary*. Unbelievable. What amazing luck, what amazing good fortune. He had heard, vaguely, about Austin Reed's on-board shops, but had never really considered working in one as a possibility for himself. He never thought in a million years he would get such a chance to travel. He could never have afforded it otherwise. Albert did a little Gene Kelly jig down the corridor, before composing himself again to go back to his rarefied post to sell.

Albert soon found out he was going, in fact, with two other employees from Nottingham, and two from Sheffield, who had been hand-picked for the cruise. Their job was to man the on-board shop across the Atlantic, and provide impeccable Austin Reed service to the elite *Queen Mary* customers, who might want a light summer suit and all the trimmings, or a new evening suit, with tails, or just a new top hat, or pair of kid gloves. Albert was utterly over the moon. A poor boy from Bulwell, going on the *Queen Mary*.

At twenty-six, he was still living at home, and when he told his parents, his father grunted, but his mother was utterly thrilled. Albert had recently had a girlfriend, Daisy, actually a fiancée, for a short time, but it hadn't worked out. His heart and confidence had been dented from this experience and he was still licking his wounds when the *Queen Mary* offer came. He had been feeling rejected and low, and wondering whether he would ever find someone special to share his life, even though he went out to socials (mainly still through the church), and also danced at the ever popular Palais de Danse. The truth was that despite being a retail salesman, he was shy with girls. He just was not particularly great at the traditional 'pick up' patter or selling himself. The offer of the trip to New York was the best antidote for a broken heart that he could possibly have.

New York was glamorous, exciting, dramatic and huge. Albert had seen it in all the films he loved: the skyscrapers, Central Park, Fifth Avenue, the Subway – and now he was treading those hallowed streets. He was with three male colleagues who had been before, luckily, and who knew the ropes. They were staying on the ship as night, so it was their floating hotel, and they were given sixty dollars pocket money for three days, which seemed a fortune to Albert, to spend on food and 'expenses'. He felt the world – or at least New York – was his oyster.

He, Albert Godfrey, from Bulwell, walked round Manhattan and stood in Times Square. He was overawed by the size of the skyscrapers, the speed of the yellow taxis and the rapid-fire talk of the New Yorkers, whom he could hardly understand. He went up the Empire State building and saw the Statue of Liberty, walked along Fifth Avenue and went to Staten Island. He and his friends enjoyed Coney Island, along with New Yorkers, ate salt beef sandwiches and drank root beer. Albert also went round the famous Macy's open-mouthed, drinking in the glorious fashions and the marvellous household goods. Then the lads hit the bars and pubs and clubs and had a whale of a time: four footloose young men in the big city (it was like *Singin' in the Rain*, after all). Albert could not get over the size of the city and the pace of life: after quiet Bulwell, even after busy Nottingham, New York was another speedy world.

Plus, the voyage itself had been wonderful. Albert had loved to hang over the wooden rail and watch the dolphins and fish leaping out of the water near the prow, as the ship ploughed its way powerfully across the huge, grey Atlantic. The ship was full of art deco splendour, with mirrors, velvets, Indian carpets, chandeliers and walnut wood, and the guests were draped in jewels and furs. Even though their staff cabin was minuscule and pressed into the bowels of the ship with four young men squished into it, Albert didn't care. The thrum of the engines was quite comforting at night, and it was warm and snug. Albert was just excited to be having such an unexpected adventure.

Albert's sales were good, and he found himself able to cope with the rough seas around the Bay of Biscay in particular, the likes of which he had never encountered before. In fact, when his colleagues were green and ailing, Albert sailed on, providing impeccable service to the most discerning of customers, which included lords and gentry of all kinds, Hollywood film stars and MPs, successful businessmen and the odd, wealthy, self-made man. The whole experience embodied absolute luxury and Albert made sure he was his most charming and attentive self while selling to well-heeled gentlemen of every creed and culture.

He did so well at sales on the trip, that he would be offered the opportunity twice more, including a trip on the *Queen Mary*'s sister ship, the *Queen Elizabeth*. He had good bonus money when he returned, which he was able to save.

For Albert, Austin Reed had been an exemplary employer, and under its tutelage, he had learned to become a top salesman. His trips to New York, manning the Austin Reed shops, were journeys of a lifetime, providing him with unforgettable experiences that he'd savour for the rest of his life.

6

Out on the Road

Back in Nottingham, word got around the retail grapevine that Albert Godfrey was an excellent salesman, and doing brilliantly. One day he received a message to meet someone in the Austin Reed reception at the end of the day. Albert was mystified, but intrigued, and discovered his visitor was none other than the manager of Richard Lunt's on Houndsgate, Mr Fisher, his first retail employer.

They went to a local pub, and Albert was sounded out for a new post. 'We now have a sales force on the road, travelling between retail outlets, and we wondered if you would be interested in becoming a commercial traveller?'

Albert was astounded. He had been at Austin Reed for nearly five years by now and had been wondering where he might go next. 'What would it entail?' asked Albert, sipping his beer.

'We would give you a company car, which will be changed every year, and a meal allowance. You would be covering the Midlands – that would be your territory, operating out of Birmingham,' Mr Fisher explained. 'You would get your board and lodging paid, and you will be on a bonus sales scheme.'

As Albert knew the Richard Lunt stock well, he knew he would be able to sell it. But it would mean a complete lifestyle change, driving between cities and towns, and selling door to door.

'Have a think,' said Mr Fisher, 'but we'd really like you to join us, Albert. We need good salesmen, like you, to join our team. The sky's the limit.'

Albert took the job not because he was fed up with Austin Reed, but because it would open a whole new horizon to him. Back in the late 1950s, the roads were largely empty and driving was quite a pleasure.

Albert took to life selling on the road with glee, and covered a huge area for Richard Lunt, selling women's clothes, including lingerie. He soon discovered there was a lot of pressure in getting from place to place on time with his Austin loaded up with at least ten brown leather cases full of the next season's garments. But on balance, he enjoyed the freedom of being a one-man-sales-band, travelling from Nottingham to Grantham, Derby, Harrogate, Birmingham, Sheffield, and even further afield, and back.

He had to keep a tally of his sales in a ledger, and at night, in his bed and breakfast or over a pint at a pub, keep tabs on his orders. Then he had to take the orders back to the Richard Lunt warehouse in central Nottingham and make sure that they were despatched. There was a lot of paperwork and a lot of driving, on top of having to be a sole trader out on the road.

On his travels, he met Pam, a sweet young woman, who was working in a fashion shop in Grantham, and there was an instant spark between them. They began to 'court' almost straight away. As Albert drove through the fields and over dales, he thought of Pam and wondered if they might make a go of it. He wanted children, to build his own family. Visiting America and seeing the commercial spirit in action had motivated him to achieve as much as he possibly could.

As he filled his order sheets and balanced his books, or set off again in the morning sunlight or grey drizzle to make more sales, Albert reflected on how far he had come. Now he was driving a new car, travelling the road, making sales, and had found a possible partner in Pam, with whom he was on the brink of building a new life. Albert thanked the Lord at church on Sunday and felt lucky for the breaks that he had been given.

7

Family Life

Always looking for a better job and more money, Albert accepted a position working for a baby clothes firm in London, and spent several more years travelling the length and breadth of the country. He was the king of sales, with a gift of the gab.

However, the hours were long and it was a tough and lonely life. Albert missed his home, his sweetheart and his community, as he went from shop to shop selling his wares. It was a 'Go West Young Man' era, but there was only so long any young man could trudge up and down the long and winding A roads.

Albert's health suffered and so he decided to resign. He rested up for a while, including a stint in hospital, where he had time to think. It was a turning point. He had been on the go, striving to better himself, for years, and now it was all catching up with him. Albert needed a break – the stress of balancing the books, meeting deadlines, driving for hours, getting back to headquarters and always 'making that sale' had pushed him over the edge. He had always wanted to do better and better, but now he looked to setting up his own family life. It was time to get off the treadmill.

He and Pam had married, and had a baby girl, and Albert now settled into family life and into helping in the local community. He knew he needed to put down roots and look after his physical and mental health, and family life provided all that he needed from then on. However, Albert was no slouch, and he wanted to give back to the community as well, and this fitted with his spiritual beliefs.

After he retired, all Albert's skills came into play, as he volunteered to drive elderly people to hospital appointments, and even used his shorthand and typewriting from his night school years to write local history articles for the local newspaper, his church magazine and for Nottingham's social history publication, *Bygones*. He's a veritable fount of Nottingham knowledge.

Always a spiritual man, Albert continues to go to church and sings in the choir, and is the one to organise school and other reunions. He is now eighty and still lives with Pam.

Pauline Braker
née Astill

Pauline selling SR toothpaste at Boots.

1

No Job for a Girl

Just a mile and a half east of Nottingham city centre lies Colwick Woods, a leafy beauty spot near the River Trent that spawned masses of red-brick council houses in the 1920s for workers moving out of the overcrowded slums, including the Meadows. Pauline's family, like Betty's and Albert's, had been offered the chance of moving out to fresher air and newer housing when she was a baby and they'd leapt at it. Pauline's father, Frederick Astill, had worked all his life as an engineer at the Raleigh in Triumph Road, in the city centre. His own father had been Jesse Boot's first errand boy (ironically riding a Raleigh bike with a basket for his deliveries).

In her teens, Bertha, Pauline's mother, had been a crane driver at the Chilwell ammunition factory when women took over men's jobs during the Great War. The women who worked long hours in the factory were called 'Canary Girls' as they turned green and yellow from the toxic chemicals, which also gave them headaches, coughs and nausea. Chilwell ammunition factory has gone done in history for the July 1918 explosion that killed 134 workers and injured 250. It was, and still is, one of the worst munitions accidents in British history. Amazingly, Bertha was only alive as she had had a cold that day and stayed home, a story that she often told her family and friends with great relish.

It was 1951, and although the Second World War had ended six years earlier, rationing was still strictly enforced. Times were incredibly tough, as Nottingham, like other British cities, was busy rebuilding itself and redefining its way of life.

Fourteen-year-old Pauline was a very unhappy girl indeed that summer afternoon. She sat on the back step of her house, crying hard into the royal blue sleeve of her school uniform. Pauline was inconsolable, even when Kitty, the black-haired family cat, crawled deep into her lap and started pawing and purring. 'It's not fair,' she told Kitty, 'it's just not fair.' This prompted another wave of wailing, and she sobbed for her shattered heart. She didn't care if she messed up her uniform, didn't care if anyone heard or if she got told off – she just didn't care about anything or anyone any more.

Bertha appeared behind her at the back door, tea towel in hand, and quietly studied her daughter's hunched back, before turning into the kitchen.

Pauline wiped her face on her sleeve again, and looked up at the sky, mottle-faced. Nature always helped to calm her down. The huge oak and ash trees, the silver birches and chestnuts, with their luscious pink and white candles, were all waving in the evening breeze. She noticed a gaggle of geese flying in formation overhead, honking dramatically. Then she remembered her plight, and her face fell. 'What's been the point of trying?' she whispered to Kitty, who was now curled up in a tight furry ball in her lap, her paw tucked over her nose. 'Why on earth did I bother, as it makes no odds.'

Pauline's mind ran back over the painful scene at teatime. She had just come home from the Jesse Boot Junior School, full of the joys of summer, hopping and skipping the whole way. Just wait till I tell my mother, she'd thought. Pauline loved school, and was always in the top three in maths and English, if not the top. She also loved reading books of any kind, geography, history, English, art, you name it – but maths was her favourite.

Pauline's mother had been busy when she'd got back after school, stoically digging the vegetable patch which surrounded the old Anderson shelter with a large garden fork. The kids often liked to play games in the shelter, as it was scary but fun, now the war was over, to go down the steps into the dank, musky darkness. Pauline had sat on the top back house step and stroked Kitty as she waited to impart her good news.

Unfortunately for Pauline, her father Frederick came home before she'd had a chance to talk to her mother. Without a word he came up the side path and went straight to the black creosoted garden shed to put his tool bag in; he was always tired after a long day's work and bus ride from the Raleigh. Pauline watched as he washed his hands at the outside tap, and then he walked past her sitting on the step and up into the house, without a word. Pauline thought he looked quite old, like a granddad really, with his cap pulled down hard over his grey hair and grizzled five o'clock shadow. Both her parents were in their forties, and her mum also seemed a bit ancient with her thick waist, salt-and-pepper hair and crêpey skin. Pauline was the youngest of four – an afterthought, or so she believed – and her sisters Eileen, Mavis and Audrey were all grown up and already at work. The two eldest had left home, but Audrey still lived in Colwick Woods, although she was 'courting' seriously.

At the tea table with her parents and Audrey, who was back from working at a Boots shop in Nottingham, Pauline knew she had to speak, but didn't know how to begin. She pushed her food around the plate: rissoles, made with the leftover pork mixed with mash from the weekend and carrots and cabbage from the garden. She chewed slowly on a chunk of carrot, trying to work out the right thing to say. She knew better than to disturb her father, especially if he was in the middle of something, like eating, as his temper usually got the better of him.

But the news was burning into her, and she wanted to shout it out.

'Don't pick at yer food, Pauline,' chided her mother. 'Don't mess about wi' it ... Waste not, want not.'

For some reason this prompted Pauline to blurt out, 'I've a place at the high school, for next year.'

Her father, still chewing, slammed his fork and knife down with a bang on the table, making Pauline jump. 'Yer what?'

Pauline was unnerved, but she had started so she might as well finish. 'Mrs Blenkinsop put me in and I've passed ... I've a place.'

Bertha paused a moment and looked like she might speak, but then carried on eating. Audrey kept her head down, chewing. No one said well done.

'Well, yer'll not tek it,' said her father, stabbing a carrot with his fork, 'I warned you before.'

Pauline looked at him, aghast, her eyes widened and she looked over to her mother for support. Surely he didn't mean it? Pauline remembered a horrible argument back in the winter, just before Christmas, when she'd brought up going on to the high school, but she'd put his refusal then down to too much beer on her father's part. Mrs Blenkinsop had said, 'Pauline you are a very good pupil, and top of the class, so I think we should put you in for matriculation.' Pauline had been over the moon.

Surely, now she had the actual result, as she'd done the work, and applied herself, that made a difference? 'Mother?' implored Pauline, near to tears, 'Mum?'

Pauline's mother put her knife and fork down but didn't meet her daughter's gaze. 'Yer dad's right,' she said in a small voice, after a pause, 'we told you before.'

Pauline's eyes spilled over and her chin wobbled, 'But Muuuuum, Mrs Blenkinsop said ah'd mek a good teacher … she said I was good at tests and she put me in … and I passed wi' flying colours. I thought yer'd be proud—'

This lit the blue touch paper, and her father exploded: 'Mrs Blenkinsop? I'll gi' you Mrs bleddy Blenkinsop. What does she know, eh? I told yer before and yer've defied us. Yer'll not go to any fancy school and that's that. There's all that blinkin' uniform to get and what not. Yer'll go and get a proper job, like yer sisters. Work's good enough fer them, it's good enough fer you.'

Audrey sat back in her chair and looked down, picking at her nails. Bertha busied herself tidying up the plates on the table.

'But why …?' cried Pauline, heartbroken. Surely this was good news for the family, that she'd found a way to go higher in life? She'd seen her father work his way up at the Raleigh, now he was in charge of quite a few apprentices and had more responsibility. He was always regaling his family with tales illustrating the need for hard graft, and told them that you didn't get anywhere without real effort. Surely it was a good thing to want to do better?

'Why? Why?' shouted her father. 'Because I said so, that's why.' He went beet red, stood up and pushed his chair back. He leaned his knuckles on the table and loomed threateningly over Pauline, who shrank back into her chair. 'I've worked at Raleigh, man and boy, these thirty year, and my father worked at Boots all his natural life, and my grandfather before him, and proper work is what yer'll do, my girl. Not teaching. Not summat high falutin'. Yer'll do real work, like the rest of us. Yer getting above yersel', yer are. Yer all kippers and curtains.' He straightened up and put his hands on his hips. 'It's no place fer a girl like yer and that's that.'

Out on the doorstep, Pauline shivered in the dusk, remembering the horrible teatime scene. So unfair. So humiliating. She'd never, ever get over it. She felt desolate and alone; so misunderstood and mistreated. She watched the evening sky coming in now in all its glory: dark indigo, crimson, orange, yellow, grey, sweeping over the fields and factories and melting over the trees and rows of chimney-clad rooftops. Pauline liked looking at the sky, the branches, the birds, the clouds, the dark silhouettes. The sky had scope, it had space, up there. Somehow in the sky there were no rules, regulations, no musts, no shoulds, no screaming matches, no shouty, nasty fathers and no silent, grumpy mothers or sulky

177

sisters who didn't care what happened to her. 'It's just not fair,' repeated Pauline to Kitty, who was still a warm fur ball in her lap. Pauline wiped her snotty nose on her already sodden sleeve with a feeling of satisfaction at the mess it had made. So there! She started counting on her fingers, counting numbers up and down, 1, 2, 3, 4, 5 ... 5, 4, 3, 2, 1, as it comforted and calmed her. She always did this to get her emotions back into check.

Eventually, Pauline peeked over her shoulder, but there was no sign of her mother in the square-paned kitchen window over the sink. This meant the teatime washing up was done (Father would never do it). A light came on in the house, which signalled that her mother was now sat in her winged armchair, listening to the wireless while doing her perpetual knitting or mending. Father would already be at the Inn on the Hill, his usual haunt. After tonight's argument, he'd come back more grumpy and difficult than ever, so she'd be sure to be out of the way. Right now, she hated them all (except Kitty, of course).

2

Weighing In

'Goodbye, Pauline, and good luck,' said Mrs Blenkinsop. 'Pop in and see us any time … I'm sure you'll be fine.'

'Bye, Mrs Blenkinsop, and thank you,' said a tearful Pauline, and started trudging home for the last time, lugging her PE bag and desk contents with a heavy heart. She took the long way home, past the palatial Colwick Hall, which was once owned by the poet Byron's family, with its Gothic chimneypots and windows, and then down a path to the River Trent, where she sat down in the leafy glade and contemplated her future. The woods were renowned for a particularly heinous murder that took place in 1844, when William Saville cut the throats of his wife and three children. 'Saville's Spinney' was named after the perpetrator who was hanged in Old Market Square in front of a crowd of hundreds. After his execution, in the crush to leave, twelve people died. Although it was a terrible event, it also gave Colwick Woods a notoriously infamous beauty spot for locals to go 'spooning', or to ponder in when times got bad.

Pauline brooded over her last week at school. The careers teacher, a Mr Bryan, had told her bluntly that leaving school without higher certificates meant one thing only: her career would be in a factory, shop or office. Or she could get married, of course, and have children. She pulled out a copy of the *Nottingham Evening Post* the teacher had given her, and turned to the back, looking at the classifieds. Her eyes blurred as she read … but soon alighted upon an advert for an 'office junior' at Avery Scales, the weighing machine manufacturers. The main office was in Lace Market, central Nottingham, and for a moment Pauline imagined herself dressed in a lovely floral dress, sitting at a desk, writing. OK, she thought moodily, I might as well give it a go.

Two weeks later, Pauline was walking along Parliament Street towards Lace Market, which was the original 'burh' or centre of Nottingham and the ancient hub of industrial enterprise. The Lace Market still had offices, factories and warehouses of every ilk, and in dark alleyways there were still lace makers and hosiers producing delicate goods. Pauline felt quite overwhelmed walking through the streets in her Sunday best French blue dress, with its white Peter Pan collar and cinched-in waist. It was her first day. She'd had an interview with a Mrs Brennan only the week before and had got the job on the spot, to her amazement.

Pauline understood she was going to work for the sales team, and that the Avery premises were a mix of warehouses and administrative offices. 'At least you are on time,' Mrs Brennan said, as Pauline arrived. Overly sensitive, Pauline instantly felt told off, until she saw Mrs Brennan smile. She realised she'd have to get to know her sense of humour: this was work, not school.

Mrs Brennan took Pauline upstairs to the typing pool, a windowless, rectangular room, where two other young women – both older than her – were tapping away furiously at their noisy metal machines that pinged every time the typewriter roller got to the end of a row.

Mrs Brennan said, 'That's Maisie and Dolores,' and both young women looked up briefly and nodded at Pauline. She said 'hello' back and blushed shyly as they went back to their work.

'And this is your desk,' Mrs Brennan said, indicating a dark cubby hole in the corner of the room, by a row of grey metal filing cabinets, beside the coat rack. Pauline's desk had a metal hole-punch and a stapler, with a dark green metal waste bin under it. She also had three wire filing trays in a stack, labelled with 'Out' at the top, 'Pending' in the middle and 'File' at the bottom. Pauline didn't know what 'Pending' meant; it was all very confusing. Then Mrs Brennan showed Pauline the stationery cupboard off the corridor and gave her some white and coloured foolscap paper (pink, yellow and blue), carbon paper, pencils, a rubber and a shorthand notebook.

Pauline must have looked terrified as Mrs Brennan walked her briskly along the corridor and sat her down in her own neat and tidy office. 'First things first. Let's get some things straight. You are to answer the telephone with "Good morning, Avery Scales", and then write down a message and give it to Maisie in your office. You are also to take dictation for the salesmen, and Mr Hillier in particular.' She waited for it to sink in. 'You'll find them in the back office, along this corridor, and you are to do what he asks you. Do you understand?' Pauline nodded, but panicked wildly underneath as she had never used a telephone. Mrs Brennan sniffed, and glanced at her watch, 'You can manage that?'

'Well, er … actually,' began Pauline, 'what's "dictation"?'

Mrs Brennan looked aghast and sighed dramatically. 'Oh, dear me, what have we got here?' She paused. 'No typing?'

Pauline felt tears welling up, as she was failing already, and she shook her head, dismally.

'No shorthand?'

Pauline bit her lip, she didn't want to cry.

'Oh dear, oh dear, that will never do,' Mrs Brennan thought for a moment, and Pauline held her breath. Well, that was it, she'd have to look again. What would her father say? She began to imagine another teatime scene and felt her heart pumping with fear.

'All right,' said Mrs Brennan decisively, popping Pauline's disastrous daydream, 'you're to go to night school to learn Pitman's and typewriting. You're to start right away, this week. Do you think you can do that?'

Pauline brightened at the idea of going to night school as the idea of learning anything at all made her day. 'Yes, of course, Mrs Brennan, I'm sure I can.'

3

The Typing Pool

The next few weeks and months went by in a blur of travelling to work on the bus and learning all her new office tasks, then going to night school twice a week. Pauline soon found out that 'office junior' really meant 'general dogsbody' as she was regularly sent on errands, fetching and carrying paper from the stationery cupboard, or filing paperwork in the battery of grey filing cabinets. She also was sent out to get buns from a local bakery, to go with the tea that she had to serve up from a huge aluminium teapot in the staff room.

Pauline was taught how the sales and invoicing system worked. She liked working with the sales team, three lively men in suits who inhabited a smoke-filled room at the end of the corridor, and they always cracked a joke with her. She enjoyed night school as she loved learning shorthand, particularly as it was so puzzle-like. The typing was not so bad and she soon found she was quite good at it.

In the daytime, Pauline had to answer the dark brown Bakelite telephone for the sales office and the typing pool, write a message on her notepad and hand it to Maisie, who would then give it back to her with instructions to take it to the appropriate person. She would often ask Maisie, the friendliest of the typists, exactly who she had to find and where they were in the warren of offices. Pauline liked going round to different people and finding out about the business. Once, she wandered into the warehouse to deliver a message and was overawed by the rows and rows of packages on metal shelves. She got teased by the lads in grey coats, 'Ayup, what've we got 'ere?' and she soon scooted upstairs again to the safety of her cubbyhole desk.

The biggest skill she had to conquer, at first, was typing. Her shorthand was coming on gradually, but it was like learning a new language and the teacher had told her it would take time. She was going to sit her first exam, taking down sixty words a minute, at Christmas, so she was studying hard. However, typewriting on her heavy, black Olympia typewriter was a much tougher exercise. The two other typists had slightly more modern, grey versions, but, as the junior, she had been given the oldest and heaviest machine. She had to learn how to change the ribbon, which was half black and half red, and fiddle to thread it carefully into the machine, getting her fingers filthy with ink in the process.

Mr Hillier, her particular salesman, had been quite friendly from the start, albeit exacting. He was a dapper little man in a pinstriped suit with a great deal of Brylcreem on his dark brown hair. He had a bushy moustache like a hairy caterpillar on his top lip, which fascinated Pauline and made her want to laugh. Not long after she started he had called her in by telephone and asked her to 'take a letter'. She had no idea what this meant, but she picked up her shorthand notebook and pencil and entered his office with trembling knees.

'Ah, Pauline, take a seat.'

Pauline sat down opposite Mr Hillier, who was almost hidden behind his desk piled high with manila folders. He was smoking a cigarette and offered her one from an ornate wooden box on his desk.

'Oh no, I don't smoke,' said Pauline, somewhat taken aback. She was only fourteen.

Only one of the other two salesmen, a Mr Jones, was in the room, also puffing away. The other was out getting an order. Mr Jones was kindly and middle-aged with wavy grey hair, and was talking loudly on his phone about a meeting. Pauline tried to ignore what he was saying, opened her notebook, crossed her legs and waited, heart racing.

'Dear sir,' began Mr Hillier, 'Thank you for your letter of the Nineteenth Inst—'

Pauline tried to keep up, and half-wrote, half scribbled a letter of muddled shorthand mixed with her own made up hieroglyphics. She wanted to ask Mr Hillier to repeat the letter, but was too frightened to ask him anything. She just hoped she would be able to decipher her scribbles enough to piece together a coherent letter.

Once back at her desk, Pauline put a piece of white foolscap paper flat on the desktop, then a piece of carbon paper, matt side down, shiny side up, then added a pink and yellow sheet, both with carbon sheets in between. She fed the whole pack of paper and carbon into the roller of her typewriter, neatly aligning the sheets, so they were straight. All this she'd learned at night school. She got ready to strike her first keys to type in the business address in the top left-hand corner of the paper. Pauline looked across the room at Maisie who was typing at machine-gun speed, and then down at her own QWERTY keys. Pauline bit her lip in concentration. She began the address, pressing down heavily on one key at a time, so each went 'clunk' onto the paper-covered roller, making a letter appear on the paper in black ink pressed through from the ribbon.

After typing the address of the recipient she rolled the paper up to check that her typing had gone through all the layers of paper and carbon, from the white sheet right through to the bottom yellow one. She knew the pink and yellow copies would be filed away in the office and the top white copy would be sent out to the recipient, so it all had to be perfect. If she made a mistake she had to correct it by hand. To do this she had special correcting fluid that she would paint on the wrong letter or word on the top white paper, and the pink and yellow filing papers underneath. She would roll the typing sheets up, release the bar that kept them all in place and paint on the correcting fluid between the sheets. To dry the liquid properly she had to blow on it, otherwise it smudged. Then she had to retype the wrong letter, to blank it out and roll the sheets of paper back down, align them perfectly, back to where they were before, and type in the correct letter. This part often went wrong.

Pauline learned very quickly that even if she wiped out the wrong letter the first time round, inserting the correct one was quite haphazard. The letter would often come out higher or lower or wonky on the top page, looking a mess. This typing lark was quite skilled work, Pauline realised, and it needed a lot of dexterity and patience. Sometimes, her hands would be shaking so much or sweating, that ink would start smearing over the top copy, which was a disaster. She often got her inky fingerprints on the top copy and would have to start the whole process all over again, even though she had her eye on the clock, as the letter would have to get into the post that day. Pauline discovered fairly soon that if she made a mistake (and hadn't corrected it properly), or if Mr Hillier changed his mind and edited the letter, she had to type another set all over again and discard the first effort.

Once she had perfected Mr Hillier's letters, she had

to place them in a large, flat black leather folder for him to sign. The pink and yellow copies were put in their respective filing trays in the typing pool, the pink going into the main filing system along the wall, for general reference, and the yellow going to the salesman's office for his reference (each salesman had their own personal filing cabinet). Then she would have to type an envelope, again getting the address perfectly aligned in its centre.

Every afternoon, Pauline walked along the corridor to Mr Hillier's desk and left the black folder on its front edge for his signature. Later, she would have to go back and collect it, in time for her to put the signed letters in their typed envelopes, lick the glue and seal them, and then get them down to the post room in the basement by 5pm at the very latest. They would all be franked by Joe and Charlie using a huge clunky machine, and then stuffed into a hessian sack stamped with 'PO' in black letters. Finally, a local postman would come and collect the sacks, throw them in his van and take them to the central sorting office in Nottingham.

Meanwhile, Pauline also had to file all the accumulated pink and yellow copies by the end of the working day. Maisie and Dolores would both be throwing copies into the trays like confetti as they worked. Pauline liked this part as it was a bit like a quiz. She would often find people had filed things in the wrong places, and she would sort them out diligently. The letters had to be filed in date order in the files, working from the back of the file forwards. There were a lot of files and products and companies to go through, as Avery made industrial scales, household scales, all sorts of things, and some of the orders were huge, some small.

By the end of the day, Pauline's desk had to be spic and span. Her blotting paper on her desk pad, which soaked up ink, had to be clear. Her typewriter was pushed to the back of the desk, and she had to put a fitted canvas hood over it to keep the dust out of the keys. Mrs Brennan would appear around 5.15 and hover around the desks. 'What's this, Maisie?' she would say, pointing to a half-typed and discarded pink copy. 'Waste,' she would say and tut under her breath.

Maisie would reply, 'Sorry, Mrs Brennan, but there was a rush on—'

'I dare say, but it's no excuses for sloppy work ...'

Pauline would feel sorry for Maisie. They were so hard-pressed in the typing pool, and nobody really understood how difficult the work could be. Pauline still felt terrified of that moment Mr Hillier would say, 'Take a letter,' or pass her desk, saying, 'Pick up your notepad and come through.'

As she sat on the bus home, travelling the short journey to Colwick Woods, Pauline watched the sky and trees and thought about the job. She still felt some bitterness about not staying on at school, but she had begun to enjoy dressing up for work and doing something important with her day. However, Pauline did find the work quite repetitive and boring. It didn't engage her brain and she still found herself day-dreaming about what might have been.

Nonetheless, she did feel proud about putting her wages on the table on a Friday night. Her mother would give her some money back so she could go out to the cinema, which she loved. Pauline also adored dancing and music and she decided, that evening on the bus back home, that she would have some dance lessons at Hanford and Richards, a popular dance school in Nottingham, now she was earning her own money.

Little did she know it was a decision that was about to change her life.

4

Boots Shop Girl

It was love at first sight. Pauline saw him across the room and thought he looked the spitting image of Dirk Bogarde in *The Blue Lamp*, all dark and moody, with slicked-back raven hair and fine, sensitive features. Pauline was particularly taken by his 'duck's anatomy' or 'DA' (his hair 'quiff'), which was sculpted with Brylcreem. She thought, as she sipped her cream soda through a straw, Oh, my goodness, he's gorgeous.

Pauline hid behind Cynthia, her best friend from school, and peeked out at him across Hanford and Richards dance hall in Trinity Walk, Nottingham. Johnnie Ray's 'All of Me' was playing loudly and Pauline envied all the dancers whizzing round the dance floor, hand in hand, in easy close proximity. Closing her eyes and swaying with the music, she willed her 'Dirk' to come over as she flattened herself against the wall, just like all the other 'wallflower' girls in their big-skirted party frocks and white bobby-socks, desperately waiting to be asked. When Pauline opened her eyes again at the end of the song, she was amazed to find her heart-throb and a couple of his friends were heading their way, swept along the with the tide of dancers. The disc now playing was Al Martino's 'Here is My Heart' and Cynthia, bolder than Pauline, flirted and smiled openly, saying a brazen 'Hello' to the likely lads. Pauline was embarrassed at first, blushing wildly, and then was amazed when 'her one' sidled over and said, 'Would yer like ter dance?'

Pauline nearly fainted. 'I'd love to,' she answered, turning an even deeper puce.

'Ahm Arthur,' said the Dirk lookalike.

'Pauline,' she replied, and then yelped 'Ow!' as he trod on her big toe.

'Oh, ahm sorry, two left feet, me,' said Arthur, truly abashed. 'Are yer all right?'

Pauline nodded and they both laughed.

'Where'd yer work?' Arthur shouted over the din.

'Avery's,' Pauline shouted back, 'in't office. Been there a year, nigh on. You?'

'Ahm at Players,' said Arthur, 'packing ciggies.'

They laughed again as Arthur trod on her other foot for good measure. For the rest of the evening, fifteen-year-old Pauline taught sixteen-year-old Arthur to dance to all her favourites records on the brand-new 'Hit Parade' which had just begun that year, 1952.

Afterwards, Arthur walked Pauline to her bus stop and, on the way, Pauline asked Arthur shyly if he would come to her sixteenth birthday party in a couple of weeks' time.

In fact, the 'party' ended up being only Pauline, her best friend and matchmaker Cynthia, and Arthur, in Pauline's family kitchen in Colwick Woods, with the radio on, a tea of Victoria sponge, Ritz crackers and soda pop, and with her parents hovering around. The three teenagers went to sit on the sofa to chat and listen to music.

It was a bit awkward being a three, as Pauline and Arthur were clearly attracted and Cynthia was playing 'gooseberry'. However, when Cynthia popped to the toilet and Pauline's parents were busy in the garden, Arthur leaned over to shy Pauline, put his arm around her, said, 'Happy birthday, Pauline,' and stole his first kiss. She asked him afterwards, would he have kissed Cynthia if Pauline had gone off to the toilet first?

'Don't be soft,' was his answer, 'Ah only have eyes fer yer, yer daft brush.'

So from that moment, they became a couple, despite Pauline's misgivings.

There were other significant changes in 1952, national as well as personal in nature. Not only did the young, pretty Queen Elizabeth come to the throne and signal the end of an era of world wars and male monarchs, but also Pauline's father, Frederick, died suddenly, aged just fifty-four years old, on Christmas Eve.

Pauline had always been used to her father being a tough, strong man who ruled the roost with an iron fist in an iron glove. He had been to the Ragged School in Sneinton before the First World War, which was fairly tough and impoverished, as was his home in St Ann's, a notoriously rough and overcrowded slum district of Nottingham. His father was a struggling tailor, and his grandfather had been an errand boy for Boots, and Frederick had a testing upbringing in a big family. Pauline had childhood memories of visiting her gran, her father's mother, in St Ann's in Alfred Street North, in a back-to-back with a 'beer off' (an off licence) on the corner. The house always smelled of the homemade bread that was proving on the old black range in the kitchen-cum-living-room. They had the ubiquitous outside lavatory with squares of newspaper cut up for toilet paper and Gran's bloomers waving on the washing line.

Amazingly, Frederick had risen from this very humble beginning to swim for Nottingham by training in the local baths in Mansfield, and had won lots of championship medals. He'd even swum the Channel in 1924 with Olympic medallist Connie Jeans (who became a Nottingham headmistress). This all took discipline, determination and strength, and they were the qualities that Frederick prized above all else. He didn't suffer fools or tolerate weakness. He had started his working life at the Raleigh when he was twelve and had become an electrician. In mid-life, he began to develop glaucoma and gradually lost his sight. This was tough for him, as his eyes were essential for his work at the Raleigh, but, even so, he soldiered on with typical tenacity, despite his foggy vision, and even led men home on foot from memory and touch when pea-souper smogs descended in winter. In his latter years, while still working as head electrician, he had become increasingly crotchety and difficult as his visual impairment took hold.

Unfortunately, for Pauline, it was hard to empathise with him, as his frustration with his illness turned him into a nasty, difficult man. Then before Pauline was old enough to understand the effects his upbringing had on his character, he suddenly had a coronary and died in Pauline's arms. She was only just sixteen, and was left feeling both bereft and confused by his death: she had hugely conflicting feelings of loyalty and grief, sadness mixed with relief.

Luckily, by this time, she had become very close to Arthur, and he helped her deal with this sad upheaval at home. Her mother wanted to move house straight away: she didn't want to stay in the family home as it was so full of memories.

'Ah can't stay 'ere,' Bertha said. 'Not after all these years.' Pauline couldn't hug her mother, as she wasn't that kind of parent and it wasn't that kind of relationship, but she mashed her tea and tried to make her feel better by getting her a *Woman's Realm* magazine, or sitting with her listening to the radio in the evening.

Sipping her tea, Pauline said, 'It's all right, mother, we can move if yer want.' She didn't really want to move at all as she loved the beauty of Colwick Woods, but she said, 'If it's what you really want, it's fine by me.'

Bertha was distraught as she had lost her husband, who she had loved dearly, despite his temper. He had some insurance and a pension, but not enough for her and her two daughters to live on, so now Bertha had to be the main breadwinner. So Pauline, Audrey and their two older sisters helped Bertha exchange her council house for smaller one in Bilborough, a less pretty Nottingham suburb.

Sometimes Pauline and her mother would go to the market at Hockley, a nearby suburb, and watch with fascination as traders sold rolls of lino or flicked carpets across the floor. The 'pot man' would hold a whole eighteen-piece tea service in his arms in a giant crockery fan and throw it up in the air and catch it with a clatter, shouting 'What am I bid fer this, ah'll giv' it yer fer ten shillin's – a real bargain.' If he didn't make a sale by the end of the day, he'd let the whole lot smash in a dramatic heap onto the floor with an enormous crash, which Pauline was appalled by – what a waste. Bertha and Pauline would go to the café at the side of the market as a treat, as Pauline loved a toasted tea cake and a cup of tea or coffee. These were rare, but special mother–daughter times.

Bertha had eight brothers and sisters, one of whom, Aunty Ada, had notably (and scandalously) run off to

Jamaica to marry a black man in 1929. Bertha had some contact with her family, but they weren't particularly close, and a widow's life was a tough one, so she needed (and wanted) to go back to work as a cleaner.

The upheaval brought about by Frederick's untimely death meant that Pauline realised it was time for a change for her, too. She was not happy at Avery Scales, as she still hated having to take dictation and feared doing the shorthand just in case she got it all wrong.

Now living in Staverton Street in Bilborough, Pauline decided to look around for local jobs. Her mother was still grieving, and finding life without Frederick very hard-going. So one morning, Pauline walked out of the house, went round the corner onto the main street, and found a branch of Boots the Chemist on Bracebridge Drive. She hovered outside for a moment, and then went in and asked a woman politely behind the wooden counter, 'Excuse me, please, are yer hiring staff?'

'Wait a minute,' said the woman, and she went off and fetched a friendly, middle-aged man in a white coat.

'Hello,' he said, warmly. 'How can I help you?'

Pauline explained her situation, and he said, 'Why don't you pop back tomorrow, at five, and we'll have a little chat?'

Next day, Pauline went back on time and met with Mr Beckett, who turned out to be the manager of the branch. After a few questions about her current job, he offered her work on the spot. Pauline was elated, and rushed home and told her mother, who was utterly relieved. Then Pauline wrote her letter of resignation as she had a week's notice at Avery to work out.

Pauline was really excited, as she would no longer have to commute daily into the centre of Nottingham on the bus. Her new job was literally round the corner from her home, where she could keep an eye on her mother. In the evenings she could meet her beloved Arthur after work and they would go for a romantic walk in the forest, or to the cinema on Aspley Lane or sit in a local coffee bar. On a Saturday they would often go to a dance at the Palais or go back to Hanford and Richards where they'd met (Arthur was slowly improving with her expert tuition), or even go to the White City Greyhound Stadium for a bet and a laugh.

Pauline felt her life was beginning to move forward as she now worked close to her home, and, despite her father's death and mother's grief, she had a wonderful boyfriend with whom she was extremely happy. She had almost forgiven her father for stopping her from staying on at school. Suddenly, it all seemed a very long time ago. It was time to move on.

5

Finding 'Mr Right'

From the start, Pauline loved working at Boots and working for her avuncular manager, Mr Beckett, was a joy. It was such a relief to her to be out of an office, working with people face-to-face, and Mr Beckett was a kind and caring man, with a great sense of humour, who really cared about his team of 'girls'. Not only did it seem part of the Boots's ethos to look after the customer, but the company also made sure staff were happy and well cared for as well. An old-fashioned paternalist, Mr Beckett took Pauline under his wing from the start. He trained her up as a shop girl and wanted her to train in pharmacy dispensing, but Pauline felt she'd had enough night school by then and wanted to enjoy her new life with Arthur. She also enjoyed the company of the other shop girls, Diane, Minnie, Joan and Celia, in particular. They all got on well and had a lot in common. Finally, Pauline felt she was using her brain – there was plenty of arithmetic to do – but was free from being tied to a desk. She was much happier all round.

The shop was full of fascinating products and remedies and it had to look attractive. 'Pauline, can you polish the soaps, please?' Mr Beckett would ask, courteously. So Pauline and Diane would set about giving all the soaps on the counter a nice little rub with a cloth to make them shine, and up would waft the scents of Yardley's Lavender Soap or Bronnley's Lemon. The counters were wooden with glass partitions and the walls of the shop were lined with wooden shelves, which went up to the ceiling, with glass-fronted cupboards at the bottom. The girls would have to keep the place spic and span, and the shelves well stocked and organised, and get out the Windolene and a yellow duster to give all the glass a good rub until it shone.

They also had a lot of laughs. In 1952 buying things like condoms or even talking about sexual matters was taboo, and there was a lot of shame and secrecy associated with anything sexual. Just over a decade later, the sexual revolution would sweep away the layers of fear and misinformation that had hung over society since Victorian times. But back in the early fifties, having sex outside of marriage was not condoned or spoken about openly as most people in Britain still went to church, and it was still considered a 'sin' to have pre-marital sex or to live together. During the war years, caution was often thrown to the wind, as the threat of imminent death or danger made sex a good, if often furtive, antidote and comfort, often aided by beer, cider or 'gin and limes'.

Imagine Pauline's surprise, then, when she discovered that Boots had a range of what was called 'prophylactics'. The articles back then were fairly ugly, heavy rubber items, packaged in a plain white box.

One day a young man of about nineteen came into the chemist. Pauline was behind the counter with her light brown hair up in a sophisticated French plait (she had learned to do this recently, and felt very suave). Minnie was also at the counter, and they both watched as the young man spent ages looking at the Pepsodent toothpaste and Vosene shampoo, which was on top of the counter. 'Can I help you?' asked Pauline, in her best shop-girl manner.

The man blushed red to the roots of his hair and couldn't look her in the eye. 'I ... er ... I ... er,' he went on for a few moments. He looked up at Minnie and to Pauline, and leaned in and whispered, 'Have you got any ... you know ...'

Minnie twigged immediately and nudged Pauline, who was still none the wiser.

'I see,' said Minnie, butting in, diplomatically. 'Do you know if you would like small, medium or large?'

Pauline still had no real idea what he was asking for, but Minnie had taken over, as she was an older, more experienced, widowed woman.

'Er, large,' whispered the man, blushing even more, looking down at his shoes.

'Wait a moment,' said Minnie, and she dropped to her knees, pulling Pauline down beside her on the floor behind the counter. 'It's prophylactics he's after,' whispered Minnie, pulling out a low drawer and beginning to rifle through.

'Yer what?' whispered Pauline back.

'He wants a rubber johnny,' hissed Minnie, 'A French letter … like this.' She showed Pauline the packet, and then opened it, pulling out an ugly, brown sausage-shaped rubber item.

'Oh!' said Pauline, non-plussed.

'And they come in three sizes …' said Minnie, beginning to giggle.

'Oh, my goodness,' hissed Pauline, catching the giggles.

All this went on at floor level, with the poor young man hovering around the shop, examining razor blades and terrycloth nappies. Then Minnie and Pauline popped up from behind the counter, and straightened their faces, although their bright eyes gave away their amused state.

'Ahem, excuse me,' said Minnie, with as straight a face as she could muster. The man beetled over and simply put his coins on the counter (he knew the price) and grabbed the packet before running out of the shop.

'He's done this before,' said Minnie, brushing the coins off the counter top, causing both girls to collapse into hysterics behind the counter.

However, after closing time that day, as they pulled down the blind on the front door, Pauline whispered to Minnie, 'Do yer think yer could tell me about, yer know …' and raised her eyebrows for emphasis.

Minnie caught on immediately, 'Oh, rubbers? Of course.'

'And any other, yer know, things I should know …' Typically, Bertha had never explained anything; it was all too embarrassing for a mother to talk to her daughter about.

Minnie looked hard at Pauline for a second. She was a pretty sixteen-year-old, going on seventeen, and Minnie knew about her passion for her Arthur, as Pauline never stopped talking about him. Pauline, like most young men and women at the time, had never had any formal sex education. Sex was not spoken about, was seen as dirty, filthy and something that had to wait until marriage. However, there were plenty of young women who found themselves 'in the family way', and many a terrible back-street abortion ended in infertility and even death before the Pill was eventually available to married women in the early 1960s. Pauline had no more idea about preventing pregnancy than she could fly, until that day when she had to serve up prophylactics at work and Minnie explained.

Most young people would kiss and 'pet' or even experience 'heavy petting' which was a euphemism for getting sexually intimate without penetration. For many, sex was simply a fumble in the back of the cinema, or a grope in an alleyway, or a passionate kiss and a 'feel' or 'touch up' on the doorstep. Few people could afford a car, but if you had one, you could have a snog, or fondle, go further or even 'the whole way' in the backseat. The local park, on the grass under a coat, was also a favourite spot for young lovers. Pauline and Arthur were passionate about each other, but also very careful. It was clear that they were deeply in love.

One day, Arthur simply said, 'Shall we get wed?' and Pauline replied, 'Oh, Arthur, yes, I'd love to.' And so it was decided that they would get engaged and marry as soon as they could afford it.

Pauline told Bertha, who was pleased for her, as Arthur was a kind, warm lad, and it meant another child off her hands to feed, clothe and house. Mothers were used to their daughters having very long engagements. At that time, young men were called up for National Service – two years of compulsory military training. Arthur was told he would be going away to the army, so this meant their marriage plans had to speed up. Pauline knew that she would have to leave work once she married, as that was the custom.

Meanwhile, at work she was having a wonderful time. Dear Mr Beckett made sure 'his girls' kept healthy and dished out their Epitone blood tonic and cod liver oil every day. He took their welfare very seriously. Boots also hosted an annual dinner and dance for the staff at the Sherwood Rooms, in the centre of Nottingham near the castle. For Pauline, this was a wonderfully glamorous event, and the girls would take great care and pleasure in buying or making their flouncy evening dresses in nylon and tulle, and pairing them with long nylon or cotton gloves and high-heeled satin court shoes.

Mr Beckett was like the warm and attentive father Pauline had never had. He was always positive and charming and believed in encouraging his staff. 'Thank yer so much,' said a happy Pauline to Mr Beckett, as they waltzed round the dance floor at one event.

'It's a pleasure, Pauline, you're a very good worker – you deserve to go far. I hope you will return to us in the future, when you can.'

Pauline felt the tears welling up as this was praise indeed.

Pauline and Arthur married when Pauline was seventeen. It was a simple ceremony in the local Register Office, with a few family and friends. After a brief honeymoon in Great Yarmouth for a couple of nights in a bed and breakfast, which was all they could afford, Arthur was off to do his National Service with the army and Pauline was heartbroken. Mr Beckett allowed Pauline to stay on although she was married, as Arthur was away serving his country, and she spent the next couple of years still working at the Bracebridge branch. She had to go to the Boots annual Sherwood Rooms summer bash alone, and she missed Arthur terribly, but at least she was keeping her mother company at home.

Bertha was now going out socially, and often went to pubs round Nottingham, and made new friends. It was still unusual after the war for women to go out to the pub alone (that was the domain of 'loose women'), but there were so many widows post-war that it carried less of a social stigma than it used to. Bertha needed company, so, a couple of evenings a week after her cleaning work, she might go to a pub, and sometimes Pauline would join her at Yates's Wine Lodge on Old Market Square, or the George and Dragon on Long Row. She also liked going to the Fox or the Corner Pin.

Arthur had to leave Players when he joined up, and after his National Service he decided to go to work for Boots in the printing works at Beeston, which was a step up money-wise. Meanwhile, Pauline had to leave Boots when he came back, and they decided to get on and start their family.

Saying goodbye to Mr Beckett and the girls was hard for Pauline. She had even been a 'poster girl', as she was photographed for an SR toothpaste advert that was going to be used nationally. Her time at Boots had been wonderful, fulfilling and fun, plus she had grown her confidence and poise. However, she was ready to start her married life, with her beloved Arthur, and it was time for her next adventure to begin: she simply couldn't wait.

6

Holding the Fort

On Arthur's return from national service, Pauline and Arthur moved into a rented flat in Hyson Green, an area just north-west of the city centre.

Although Boots had a strict policy about employing married women, Pauline discovered that Players were less discriminating as workers came and went all the time, so she got a job there as she wanted to contribute to the household financially while they tried for a baby.

It was Pauline's first experience of factory life and she was put onto packing cigarettes. It was incredibly noisy and uncomfortable. She had to wear a white overall and tie up her fair hair in a bun. Her job was to sit at a conveyor belt as the tipped and untipped cigarettes flowed along like a brown and white stream, scoop them up and pop them into a hopper to pack them. Pauline found herself mesmerised as the cigarettes flowed by. She worked in a team of six, of all ages, from teenagers to eighty. The belt was noisy, as was the huge workshop, and the women worked without talking, as instructed by their strict overseer, Mrs Matthews.

Pauline was shocked at how boring the work was. She was someone who needed to use her brain, and watching the cigarettes wobble their way along the conveyor belt almost drove her mad. It was utterly mindless. The combination of this and the noise was hard for her to bear. The only really exciting part of the day was if the machine jammed – then there was a bit of drama as the mechanic came along and sorted it out, and the girls could go for a breather, or a tea-and-ciggie break.

Mrs Matthews, a stocky woman in her fifties, kept a gimlet eye on Pauline, and one day, soon after she started, she came along and whispered in her ear, 'Want to do summat different?'

Pauline's eyes brightened. The mind-numbing boredom of sitting at the conveyor belt was driving her crazy. 'Oh, yes, please,' she said gratefully.

'Come wi' me, then.' Pauline slipped off her stool and followed Mrs Matthews obediently, quite excited by the prospect of a change. 'How're yer wi' figures?'

'I like 'em,' said Pauline, brightly. 'I used to work at Boots, on t' counter.'

'So ah gather … ah could see yer was bored. All right,' said Mrs Matthews, taking Pauline through to a stock-taking area at the back of the factory floor. It was a huge room, packed floor to ceiling with boxes of cigarettes. 'Yer need to count these boxes onto a pallet, and then work out how many cigarettes are being loaded each time.'

Pauline nodded. At last her brain was being engaged. 'And yer need to notice if they're tipped or untipped, and what brand, like Senior Service, or whatever ... and mek a stock list.' She paused for a reaction, but Pauline was listening hard. 'Got it?'

'Got it.'

Mrs Matthews stomped over to the side table and brought back a clipboard and pencil. 'See this list, you must keep a proper record ... all right?'

Pauline's heart lifted. She was counting again, she was happy – anything to do with figures, numbers or arithmetic made her joyful. She needed to use her mind. Her prayers had been answered: this was so much better than watching reams of cigarettes wobble by noisily on a conveyor belt. 'I'll do my best,' she said with a huge grin. Mrs Matthews nodded sternly, not knowing that she had saved Pauline from months of mental meltdown through utter boredom.

Not long after they were married, Pauline fell pregnant. She continued to work at Players, and was happy counting the cigarettes until her son, Steve, was born.

Hyson Green was a pleasant place to live, with a little high street and shops, and as Pauline pushed her Silver Cross pram along the pavement and bought her groceries at the Co-op, she felt she was the happiest woman alive. She loved her husband dearly, loved being a mum, and felt her life had taken a new, fulfilling turn.

A second son, Andrew, followed fairly soon after, and the couple had wonderful summer days out at Trent Bridge, or a week's holiday at Trusville or Mablethorpe, family resorts that they travelled to by train. They also took their young children to the new Butlin's Holiday Camp for a week at Skegness (which seemed like paradise), or to Great Yarmouth, to stay in a caravan or lodge for bed and breakfast.

Pauline and Arthur were happy in each other's company, laughed a lot, and seldom argued. Neither of them were heavy drinkers, although Arthur did smoke, but that was common then. After her time at Players, where she came home smelling like a bonfire and couldn't get the tobacco smell out of her clothes and hair, Pauline was somewhat averse to cigarettes, but she loved her Arthur, so was tolerant of his daily habit.

Little did Pauline know that Arthur had had rheumatic fever as a child, and had been left with a heart defect. Arthur had been through the army, but had failed to tell the medics about his condition, as he had just put it down to childhood disease and not really relevant. However, his heart was weakened, and his smoking was not helping his health, despite him being a seemingly fit young father of two.

One evening, Pauline was in the flat fretting that Arthur was so late home. He was never late, as he was a real homebody, and not one to go to the pub with the lads after work. Finally, the telephone rang. It was someone from Boots at Beeston. Something had happened to Arthur and he was in Nottingham General. Pauline threw on her coat, grabbed the children and rushed to the hospital as fast as she could on the bus. When she got there she saw her poor Arthur, pale and unconscious, hooked up to a drip, in bed. Beside him was another man, another Arthur, who worked with him in the print room at Boots.

'Ayup,' he said, gently getting to his feet. 'Reckon he'll pull through.'

Pull through? Pauline looked at him aghast. 'What 'appened?'

'It were this mornin',' the elder Arthur explained. 'Me and my mate, Alan, were leaving our shift, when we saw your Arthur keel over. He just went down like a ten pin, walking through the grounds.'

Pauline clamped a hand to her mouth and her eyes filled with tears. 'Oh, no.'

'Luckily, Alan could do first aid, and, well, he saved his life – he giv' 'im the kiss of life.'

Pauline burst into tears. Her two boys sat silently and looked confused at their mother's extreme reaction. It seemed Arthur had had a massive heart attack and had nearly died on the spot. Indeed, he had stopped breathing and was turning blue. They had called to a passing member of staff to call an ambulance, and then set about saving Arthur. Their quick actions had made all the difference to his chances. Pauline could feel her knees collapsing under her, and Arthur helped her sit down, moving the boys to one side.

'Yer better see the doctor,' he said gently. 'Ah'll 'ave ter go now.'

'Thank you, so much,' said Pauline, grateful but distraught. 'Ah can't thank yer enough.'

In fact, the story made it to the local paper afterwards, and both Arthur and Alan were hailed as local heroes.

Sadly, this was the beginning of years of gradual decline for Arthur. Due to his weakened heart from childhood rheumatic fever, he would go on to have four more heart attacks.

Boots, however, being a caring, paternalistic employer, let Arthur continue working on a part-time basis. This meant that Pauline had to go back to work to earn enough money for the family to live on, and, from then on, Pauline would work nights, evenings and daytimes whenever and wherever she could. She had to hold the fort, like it or not.

She went to work in Marks and Spencer in central Nottingham, and trained in retail. She sold women's jumpers, and spent ages folding them up and placing them flat on the long counters, as that was how they were displayed then. One of the perks of working at Marks and Spencer was getting staff discount on food, which helped the family finances, and health checks for herself. Pauline was lucky to have another lovely boss, a Mr Dennis, a very benign and encouraging man who bought presents for her children at Christmas and made sure Pauline received her due in bonuses. He would give her home-made chocolates as a birthday present.

Pauline needed to earn more, however, to keep the family afloat, and in the evenings she often worked shifts in pubs, clubs, at the Greyhound racing track and even in betting shops (using her maths again). At first, Pauline's mother helped out when she could with child-care, but was ailing herself. Quite often, life would be fraught if Arthur was poorly, or needed to be home in bed, or just resting.

One day, Pauline saw that a lovely old lingerie shop, Johnston's on King Street in Chapel Gate, central Nottingham, was offering the post of manageress.

It was a traditional ladies' underwear shop, and Pauline left Marks and Spencer, and trained as a corsetière. Her head for figures, in all senses of the word, came in handy, as she had to measure women up and recommend the best product for their particular shape and purse. She had to memorise the stock, and know every corset, every bra, every size.

There was some of the original city wall under the shop, and a glass floor, where customers could look at it – it was slightly unnerving, but quite exciting. Pauline thought it was fascinating to see a little bit of Nottingham's history just there, under the floor. She also thought the shop was haunted by 'Henry' the ghost as it was always chilly and spooky in the basement storeroom.

Pauline loved this job, as it was all about giving personal service to each customer. She had always enjoyed face-to-face contact with people and the job gave her a chance to use her brain. She realised that most women were walking around in bras that just didn't fit properly at all, and she was somewhat bemused by her newfound ability to assess women as they passed her on the street in Nottingham and think, Hmmm, for goodness sake, yer could definitely do wi' coming to us for a good measure up, as she could see them flopping about in ill-fitting garments.

The job was very satisfying for Pauline as she was also responsible for balancing the books for the shop. At home, she ran the household accounts, and prided herself on the fact that they were never in debt. Indeed, she used all her skills to hold the fort while Arthur made the best recovery he could, and her two boys went to school. Pauline knew she had a lot of responsibility on her shoulders, but felt, for her family and her precious Arthur, she would always do all she could, come rain or shine.

Arthur died at only forty after a long bout of cancer treatment. Pauline never got over the loss of her beloved husband but had to soldier on for her boys. She was resourceful, and tried her hand at all sorts of jobs. There were plenty of opportunities in Nottingham at the time, but eventually Pauline went back to Marks and Spencer, where she stayed for years, benefitting from the perks, which helped her as a single mum.

Although she retired at sixty, Pauline still loves to keep her mind active; she reads, does quizzes and goes to bingo once a week. Once a year she goes on a cruise as a craft teacher with one of her friends. She loves playing with her grandchildren and tells them wonderful stories about the old days in Nottingham. Her only regret is that her lovely Arthur is not by her side.

Doreen Rushton

née Ward

Doreen in a Mablethorpe pub.

1

Father's Drunk Again

The village of Netherfield sprung up in 1846 as a frontier railway town, when Robert Stephenson built the section of the Midland Railway that connected Nottingham to Lincoln. By the end of the nineteenth century there were three railway lines going through Netherfield, all managed by the Great Northern Company. It was home to the Colwick Locomotive Depot, or the 'Colwick Loco', as it was known by locals, and a railway goods yard. By then, hundreds of red-brick terraces had been built to house the workers.

Netherfield was also a mill town, as the entrepreneur Samuel Bourne, encouraged by the excellent railway transportation for goods and labour, built a huge cotton mill there in 1883. There was a pub popular with the rail workers, aptly called the Railway Hotel, and it was outside this worthy establishment that a slight eight-year-old girl, Doreen Ward, was standing in the spring twilight in 1952.

Doreen stood outside the pub's oak front door with its mottled glass and faded gold lettering and gathered her courage. Suddenly the door burst open and a man lurched out, so Doreen scuttled past and stood inside the entrance to the bar beside a heavy red curtain, peering into the smoky gloom. It took a moment for her eyes to adjust: there were shapes of men in work clothes, still in their caps, hunched over wooden tables or standing at the bar, nursing pints of Everard's Old Bill or Kimberley Ale. A sweaty, malty smell, mixed with cigarette and pipe smoke, filled Doreen's nostrils and made her eyes water. She could hear coarse laughter and the thrum of male chat as she tried to make out a familiar figure – her father.

Doreen hovered by the door in a ragged floral dress handed down to her by one of her sisters, amazingly undaunted for someone so young. She had been sent to find Father, and find Father she would. Her older sisters found it too intimidating a task, but Doreen was fearless. She took a deep breath and dived into the dingy den, stepping around the men's legs and seated backs, taking quick peeks at their flushed faces. Doreen got some strange looks, and even a few pokes with fat fingers or jokes with rude tongues, but she ignored them, intent on her mission. Eventually, she found a familiar pair of battered boots propped up on the brass foot rail at the bar. She recognised the shabby brown corduroy trousers and, although the men were supping their pints with an absorbed air, Doreen was undeterred.

'Da-aaaaad!' She tugged at the brown corduroy trouser leg, 'Da-aaaad, Da-aaaaaaad. It's me!'

Without a word, her father slammed his pint down hard on the bar spilling some beer, grabbed Doreen by her spindly arm and, with his tungsten grip, pulled her roughly out of the pub. He threw her onto the cobbled street, and she stumbled. 'Whaddya want?' he spat out, furiously.

Doreen got up, brushed off her skirt, and stood facing her father. 'Mam's sent me fer some money,' she piped up, bravely.

Doreen noticed her dad was swaying slightly in the twilight. Grumpily, Wilfred dug around in his pockets and produced a fistful. He held out his hand, like he was feeding a horse, revealing some big brown pennies, three-penny bits, silver shillings and sixpences, which Doreen grabbed and counted. She squinted up at her dad, who was dragging heavily on his roll-up. 'It's not enough – she wants five pound.'

'Wants dunt get,' slurred her father. Nonetheless, he dug deeper in his pocket again with one hand, and threw some coins on the ground. Doreen dashed after them like a little whippet, and by the time she'd scrambled to her feet her father was already gone – back into the pub.

With her father's coins clenched tightly in her little fist, Doreen ran all the way home to their two-up-two-down terrace on Bourne Street, with Bourne's Cotton Mill looming large at the end of the road. She deposited her gleanings on the kitchen table and her mother, Lily, counted them quietly onto the maroon chenille cloth. 'Three pound and a bit,' said Lily sadly. 'Fer a week.'

Doreen looked at her mother's sloping shoulders and crushed demeanour and thought hard. 'Mebbe we can ask our Mary?' Although Doreen's sister still lived at home, she was working at Boots in Nottingham.

Lily shook her head and counted the money out again, just to make sure. 'It'll be bread and dripping again fer tea ...' Doreen's mother went to the sideboard, took a small loaf out of the white enamel bread bin and cut a thick slice onto the breadboard. She dipped a knife into a white basin, covered the bread with the dark brown dripping, and handed it to Doreen. 'Now go on wi' yer, me duck.'

Doreen hesitated briefly, and then grabbed the bread and dripping and ran out of the front door straight onto the cobbles outside. She sat on the kerb in the gloom, watching the local boys play football and girls skipping, and ate her tasty reward. Inwardly, she cursed her father: she hated her dad, hated the pub, hated smoke and grime, and especially hated drink. The bread was soon gone, but Doreen was still famished. She licked her lips and sighed, watching men strolling home in dribs and drabs – some in straight lines, some rolling and singing, some plodding – all from the evil Railway Hotel.

2

Not Wanted

Wilfred Ward was a steam train driver working for the London and North Eastern Railway Company (LNER) and needed to live in Netherfield as it was in his 'call out' area for jobs. He was extremely proud of the fact he'd driven the *Flying Scotsman* once on a long-distance journey from Scotland to London. Wilfred also regaled his family with a story of having to stop a runaway train, which he did by taking it off the main line and crashing it into a goods train. He was a bit of a local hero as a consequence.

Wilfred and Lily had already had seven children when Doreen, their last child, was born in 1944. They were in their forties and had been together for over twenty years. Doreen was told she'd been born with the umbilical cord wrapped round her throat three times, and that she'd been slapped 'black and blue' to get her breathing properly. Doreen suffered with asthma and bronchitis all her childhood, possibly from the nature of her birth. The seventh child had been stillborn a year before Doreen was born. The family didn't celebrate the dead child's birthday. Doreen's mother and father ignored the fact the child had ever existed. He 'wasn't counted', and the couple would say they had seven children, not eight. A baby simply wasn't considered as a real child if it died before being twenty-four hours old.

There was Jack, the eldest, who had already gone off to the army and fought in the Second World War. He was the one most like their father – he was tough like him – but Wilfred himself was injured in the First World War and couldn't join up. When Jack came out he went down nearby Gedling Pit as a miner.

Doreen's eldest sister, Marjorie, had already left home and was married with children in 1952. Then came Wilfred junior, who was a photographer's assistant in a Nottingham shop, then Alan who was apprenticed to an electronics firm, and Mary who was already working as a shop assistant in Boots. Gill was still at school, but would soon be working as a textile machinist in a Nottingham factory. Wilfred junior, Alan, Mary and Gill still lived at home.

When he was home, Jack would bully Doreen, the youngest, remorselessly with: 'Yer not wanted', 'Yer trouble' or 'Yer not one of us'. Or even, cruelly, 'Yer were a mistake – look what the cat's brought in.' Luckily, Doreen knew her mother loved her, even if she was not that demonstrative, and her two elder sisters, Gill and

Mary, protected her, so she would take what Jack said, in his spiteful, scapegoating way, with a pinch of salt.

Doreen could sense, without being able to understand it, that her parents were not at all happy together by the time she came along. Back then it was impossible for Lily to divorce Wilfred, as she had no money and no family. The alternative to marriage was destitution, so she put up with his temper – and worse – to keep the peace. Wilfred and Lily's characters were polar opposites, chalk and cheese, and they argued a great deal. 'Why d'yer drink all'us money away?' Doreen could hear her mother complaining late on a Friday night.

'Shuddup, yer moany bitch,' she'd hear in an angry, deeper voice, followed by a slap or a thud.

Wilfred had a terrible temper and he would take it out on Lily constantly, especially after the pub turned out. Doreen and her siblings knew their mother felt their father's fists regularly and Lily would appear in the morning with bruises, black eyes, and sometimes was admitted to Nottingham General with sprain, or even broken limbs.

When the children were all younger, if Mother was 'away' in hospital, Wilfred attempted to cook, making odd-looking burned offerings, such as sparrow or blackbird pie, which the children ate without complaining. Or he cooked with whatever he had run over with the train. He recounted stories (especially in the pub) of hitting the odd duck on the line, slowing the train down, and stopping to pick it up and take it home for tea. The children had to eat anything he produced or they got the back of his hand – or worse, his wide leather belt across their faces or rears. Mostly the children scavenged what they could, as if Mother was away, Father was down the pub, inevitably.

Indeed, Wilfred went to the Railway every day after work, where he'd down eight or ten pints of 'Old Bills', then weave his way home and finish off with black market Green Goddess Absinthe (a drink based on wormwood that was banned for some time abroad, as it was renowned for driving people insane). He was often the worse for wear, becoming violent and abusive, and when he was in this state, all the children knew they could hardly breathe in his presence without repercussions. Sometimes, when he lost his temper with Lily or one of the children, Doreen would be sent to fetch a neighbour, or Ern, who was Marjorie's husband, to pull Wilfred off his victim.

One night, when Doreen was about six, her father was drunk and arguing with Alan, her youngest brother, when Wilfred pulled out a knife, and threatened his son. Doreen was terrified, but, like the plucky soul she was, threw herself between them to protect Alan. Her father picked her up and threw her against the wall. Alan ran away, never to return. Distraught, Doreen wandered the streets for weeks looking for him, and eventually found out he had gone to Wales. Outraged, Doreen took it on herself to be the family champion, and often stood up to her father, to her other siblings' amazement, as she was the youngest. One day she said 'damn' to him, and he grabbed her by the hair, pulled her to the kitchen sink and washed her mouth out viciously with bitter carbolic soap. Then he shoved her head under the tap and turned it full on, drenching her with icy water, for good measure.

Doreen was traumatised, but not broken; his treatment of her only hardened her resolve to help others less fortunate than herself. She was often her mother's protector, or her sister's saviour, and during one family row she picked up her father's metal torch and threatened him back with it. 'Yer hit me and ah'll hit yer back!' she cried.

'Why yer little cheeky beggar!' shouted her father. 'C'mere – I'll show yer what's what.'

But Doreen was too quick. She ducked under his arm and ran out the house and down the alleyway, and was soon far away, over the railway bridge, out of his grasp. By the time she came back, he was at the pub, so she nipped upstairs, got into bed and was fast asleep by the time he rolled home.

3

Nowt Queer As Folk

Before her marriage, Lily had worked at Bourne's Cotton Mill at the end of the road, and now worked occasional shifts at the local bakehouse or at the Cornerhouse Café. She was mainly a full-time mother, and usually didn't have time for paid work. She was a good cook, however, and tried to make food stretch, making her own bread, puddings, hotpots and broth. She taught her daughters to cook and Doreen could already make jam tarts and bread at eight. Lily also was a dab hand at cutting down clothes, and was constantly altering garments on the family's treadle Singer sewing machine. Luckily, Wilfred could fix the machine when it went wrong, as he had a feel for things mechanical – if he was so minded. He also brought in bits of engine to tinker with, leaving oil over the living room, to Lily's horror.

Lily and Wilfred came from very different backgrounds: her family were quiet, orderly Methodists, and Lily would take some of the children to chapel every Sunday. Wilfred was a diehard atheist and didn't approve. 'What yer going to that bleddy place fer,' he would snipe at them, as they left for church. Lily wouldn't say anything back as she knew better than to provoke his temper. Doreen liked going with her mother, Gill and Mary, as it was a peaceful experience, and a real relief from being at home.

Wilfred, on the other hand, came from a strangely unconventional background, which probably explained his irascible nature. His mother worked at the Playhouse as a dresser to the stars, and, in particular, a popular music hall act called 'Old Mother Riley'. Old Mother Riley was, in fact, a man, Arthur Lucan, who dressed up as an Irish washerwoman, sang popular songs and told risqué jokes. Wilfred's mother was a harsh, bitter, woman. Although not religious, she was strangely superstitious – for example, not allowing green objects in the house (quite a popular idea at the time). Whenever Doreen met her she was frightened by her, as she had a dark, mysterious presence. She never smiled, never gave gifts and always criticised. On one visit to her rented rooms near the theatre, Doreen saw a voodoo effigy with pins stuck in it, which terrified her. She didn't like being alone with her grandma and begged her father not to take her again. Grandma Ward was also a gambler and won quite often, to the local bookie's chagrin. She was even banned from putting on bets by some establishments, as she was canny, and they accused her of having a crystal ball (which she might well have had).

Wilfred's mother had told him that he was the progeny of a lord who had been disinherited as he had consorted with a chorus girl (clearly Wilfred's mother, when younger). However, Doreen and her siblings whispered to each other that they thought she was probably a shamed unmarried mother, something that was seen as hugely sinful at the time. The theatre was thought to be an immoral place, as the popular Noël Coward song 'Don't Put Your Daughter on the Stage, Mrs Worthington' attested. Being an actress, or even just working in the theatre, was tantamount to being a prostitute, and it was likely that Wilfred's background and upbringing held some unsavoury truths and experiences.

Whatever his origins, Wilfred's childhood left him unwilling or unable to be nurturing and paternal, despite having so many children. He couldn't easily tolerate Lily, who was teetotal and despised the 'demon drink', and he hated her religiousness, which seemed to prompt a great deal of his ridicule and violence.

With so many mouths to feed, the family was extremely poor, and the house was part of a slum with no running water, a lavatory in the back yard, and just a cold tap in the kitchen. The children had a weekly bath in front of the fire in the main room, with the water being heated on the range. Their lighting was a mixture of gas lamps, electric (one bulb) and candles. The kitchen had the usual black range, which was a devil to keep clean with Zebrite. In fact, from a very early age, Doreen was sent off down the road to clean neighbours' ranges for a few pennies. She didn't mind sweeping the floor or cleaning the windows, as she was helping her poor mother out. If they ran out of coal (which they often did), Doreen and Alan would take an old pram and push it up Carlton Hill and see if they could pick some up from a coal yard. They were expert scavengers and good at finding things they needed and getting them for free, from scrumping apples to picking up kindling.

It was now 1953 and the entire country was full of excitement about the coming coronation of the young queen Elizabeth on 2 June, and Netherfield was no exception. The Wards had an old Bakelite Ecko radio, which stood on the sideboard, but no television. However, one of the neighbours had rented one, and when the bunting went up in the street the whole family was invited in to watch the ceremony. Doreen was now nine, and had never seen a television before as hardly anyone had them. She loved seeing the horses, the carriages and the grandeur of it all, and sat, open-mouthed, at all the people in London waving their Union Jacks and cheering. She was at the local infant and junior school at Netherfield in Ashwell Street, and they had drawn pictures of the crown jewels and the Queen, and hung up bunting there as well. There was a street party, and although rationing was still on, her mother made a cake, and the whole road came alive with singing and celebration.

Wilfred still went to the pub, mumbling, 'Bleddy monarchy, who needs 'em, waste of bleddy money, if yer ask me.'

But Doreen paid him no heed. Without him around, her mother was more relaxed and could enjoy the party without wondering if she had accidentally said or done the wrong thing. And Doreen could enjoy it too. They didn't have much – her family had hardly anything in fact – but nonetheless she felt a burst of happiness. Here she was, sitting at a trestle table with her family, friends and neighbours around her, knowing that in other parts of Netherfield, and in Nottingham, and up and down the country too, for that matter, other girls and boys her own age were sitting at tables just like this one, all of them celebrating the coronation of their pretty young queen. Even to her young mind it felt like the end of something dark and harsh, and the beginning of something fresh and new, and she looked forward to what the future might bring.

4

Standing Up to Bullies

As Doreen got older she found her fighting experience at home stood her in good stead as she was able to defend herself well against boys. Small for her age and thin, she was nonetheless wiry and strong, with a feisty disposition. At school she had a friend, Susan Makin, who had been disabled by childhood polio and got picked on by the boys. The girls and the boys played in separate areas, but the boys would come over the wall and pinch her tennis balls during a game of 'two balls up against the wall', which was popular at the time.

'Hey, what d'yer think yer doing?' Doreen would shout in the face of Peter, a schoolyard bully.

'What does it look like, skinny?' he'd shout, snatching the two balls and jumping up over the wall, 'Can't catch me.'

'Oh, can't I? Just yer watch me,' and in revenge, Doreen would hop deftly over to the boys' side where they were playing marbles and put her foot over the marble hole on the ground so they couldn't flick their marbles in. The boys were furious and tried to pull her foot off, but

Doreen stayed put, defiant. 'Gimme them balls back, an' yer can 'ave yer marbles.'

'Thank you, Doreen,' Susan would say gratefully, when they were back over their side of the playground together, safe from the bullying boys.

'It's nowt,' Doreen would say, 'ah can't stand bullies.'

Unfortunately, the teachers were not much better. Mr Blackburn would be writing on the blackboard in the arithmetic lesson and would suddenly throw the blackboard rubber backwards into the classroom, hitting an unsuspecting pupil on the head at their desk.

'Ouch,' said the innocent, but hurt pupil.

'Well, that'll stop you blathering,' the teacher would say, without turning round.

Mr Sullivan, the deputy head, took delight in breaking his ruler on his pupils' heads, hands and arms, 'Be quiet!' he would shout, spitting. 'Silence!'

Doreen would sit straight up in her chair, hoping against hope that she wouldn't be hit. She had enough of it at home. But if anyone touched her friend, Susan, she would attack back, with unbridled fierceness, not fearing the consequences.

Doreen missed a great deal of school. Moving to the secondary school in nearby Gedling when she was eleven, she missed a lot of school, for three main reasons: first, she had to fill in for her mother whenever she was hospitalised after one of Wilfred's violent outbursts; second, she would be told to go and help Marjorie, her eldest sister, with her children. She would have to wash and feed her nieces and nephews, pay the bills and do the housework, just like at home. And, third, she had asthma, which was particularly bad in winter, and she had to stay home for weeks because of violent coughing attacks. Nonetheless, Doreen loved school and loved learning new things. In particular, she liked geography, history and biology, despite the large classrooms of forty children and the punitive teachers. She was quick, and picked things up, but had huge gaps in her knowledge and homework was hard to do, due to everything that was happening at home.

Doreen liked looking after people – like her mother when she was hurt, or Marjorie's children, or her friend Susan – and the idea gradually formed in her mind that she would like to be a nurse when she grew up. She knew that she would have to go to work soon, as her brothers and sisters had done. Most of them had left school at fourteen, so she knew she would have to decide where she was going and what she should do.

One day at school, she was called into the classroom and stood before Mrs Jones, the careers officer, who sat looking at a sheet of paper in front of her. 'So, Doreen, I can see a lot of absences here.'

'Ah, yes, Mrs Jones,' said Doreen. 'Ah've been sick, and helping me mother and sister.'

'Hmmm,' said Mrs Jones, and shuffled some papers

around on her desk. 'You've not done that well. Your English could improve, and your arithmetic.'

Doreen swallowed, not knowing what to say, 'Ah like lessons, ahm sure ah can catch up.'

'Well, what do you think you want to do, Doreen?'

At that, Doreen poured out her heart, saying she'd love to be a nurse.

Mrs Jones pursed her lips. 'Oh no, it's out of the question,' she said, dismissively, 'your grades are far too poor.'

'But ah want to look after people,' implored Doreen. 'Ah can cook, ah can garden, ah like people …'

Mrs Jones wasn't listening. 'Here it is,' she said, finding a piece of paper and handing it to Doreen. 'This'll suit you. It's working at Boots. In the warehouse in the Meadows.' Doreen looked at Mrs Jones, then down at the paper. 'It's a job, regular money,' said Mrs Jones. 'It'll suit you down to the ground.'

'But Mrs Jones …' began Doreen, utterly crestfallen. She was desperate to train as a nurse, it was all she wanted to do.

'No "ifs" or "buts", it's a job, Doreen,' Mrs Jones sniffed. 'Beggars can't be choosers, you know.'

5

Boots Warehouse Worker

'Doreen, can yer move twenty of those dog-food boxes to the loading area?' said Eddie, the supervisor in her section of the Boots warehouse, which was in London Road in the Meadows area of Nottingham. 'Then come back and sort out that little lot.' Eddie was pointing across the warehouse to a huge pile of boxes full of dog biscuits and cans of dog meat, which were forming a little cardboard tower.

Doreen, in her brown button-through long-sleeved overall, jumped to it. She got hold of a platform trolley, and pushed it with some effort to the side of the huge warehouse, which was like a giant aircraft hangar with metal shelves going the length of the room and up to the ceiling. Located beside Nottingham Canal, the building was spread over several stories, with eighty staff.

Doreen got to her pile of boxes and, although they were heavy, she managed to load six onto her trolley single-handedly.

'Want a 'and?' shouted out flame-haired Sylvia, from a few feet away.

'Nah, ahm all right,' shouted back Doreen with a brave smile and a jokey grimace.

She carried on pushing her trolley-load across the room, rattling over the cement floor, and out through double doors, down a slope to the loading bay where the royal blue-and-white Boots delivery vans of various shapes and sizes were lining up.

'Ayup, 'ere comes trouble,' teased Bill, one of the drivers, hanging around his van, smoking a cigarette.

'None of yer lip,' Doreen teased back, trying to halt her runaway trolley with all her might. ''Ere gis a 'and wi' this lot then, it's fer yer van.'

'Can't yer do it yersel'?' Bill said with a grin. 'Too weedy?'

''Course, I can,' said Doreen, bristling, but good-naturedly. 'Ah've got a load more to come yet, so you'd better jump to it.'

Doreen, now sixteen, had been working in the warehouse full-time since the previous autumn, after she'd finally left school. At this time, Betty was still working at Cellular Clothing down the road; Pauline was in a Boots shop in Bilborough; and Derek was managing a Nottingham branch of Boots – although none of their paths ever actually crossed.

The work in the warehouse was laborious and boring. Doreen's job was in the pet food and sundries section and she had to memorise all Boots's products in this vast area, which she found very taxing.

Doreen easily made new friends, and soon had two good mates, the flame-haired Sylvia and Margaret. Doreen had to pack boxes with Boots's goods to fill orders, and she, Sylvia and Margaret would often stand together by the metal shelves or the wooden packing table and work as a team. It was very cold in winter, and too hot in summer, but they kept each other amused with jokes and chat. Both Sylvia and Margaret were just in their twenties, but seemed so much older to Doreen. She felt lucky to have come across such lovely women, as they were happy to show her the ropes.

'Don't pay any attention to the lads when they josh yer,' advised Sylvia on one of Doreen's first days. 'They don't mean owt. It's just their way.'

'And don't gi' Eddie any lip back,' suggested chestnut-haired Margaret. 'And don't swear.'

'Oh, ah don't swear,' said Doreen, quickly. 'Ah wouldn't. Ah don't like it.'

'Yer'll be fine then, ducks,' said Sylvia, protectively.

'But yer must be on time,' continued Margaret. 'And yer must clock in, or yer pay'll be docked summat rotten.'

Margaret had been a Land Girl during the war, and so Doreen took what she said quite seriously, as she clearly knew how to handle herself. Doreen took everything in but she was sorely tested, as the men who worked in the warehouse constantly told rude jokes, wolf-whistled or made comments about her looks or her body, and she desperately wanted to tell them off. At first she did, but she got even more teasing back, so she learned to bite her lip and keep her mouth shut. Doreen would complain about it to Margaret and Sylvia, but they'd say, 'Yer could tell Eddie, m'duck, but nobody likes a snitch,' so Doreen learned she had to keep quiet. Her experience of her brother Jack and the boys at school was useful, as she knew bullies loved it when they got a reaction, so she tried hard to ignore them and to play it cool.

Doreen took her wages home to her mother every Friday, who was extremely grateful to have the extra cash. Wilfred's drinking seemed to be escalating out of control, and his fists were equally as challenging, so her mother relied on Doreen to help her out financially as much as she could. Being an employee meant that Doreen was eligible to have a discount on some Boots items, which helped out the family even more.

There were other things about working for Boots that Doreen really liked, including a surgery that employees could go to if they had any physical complaints (even period pains, where ailing female employees got a hot water bottle and could lie down). Doreen was still vulnerable to asthma, and working in the warehouse too strenuously, or in the cold, could bring on an attack through over-exercise or dust, so knowing there was a doctor on hand at work was very reassuring. Nonetheless, she had to be careful, especially in winter when it was damp and foggy.

There were also green apples available at break time for a few pennies. It seemed very sophisticated to her to have apples on sale at work. Before she had started at Boots, Doreen had only ever eaten a couple of bananas and an orange once or twice, as fruit was still a rarity and expensive. She had scrumped apples and plums from the local allotment in Netherfield – she was a good tree climber when no one was looking. When she was younger, she and her rufty-tufty street gang and tree climbers called themselves 'The Dead End Kids', based on a popular New York stage musical of the time. Doreen was always a bit of a tomboy.

At Boots, employees were eligible to go to the social club, which had been built by Jesse Boot originally as a large Victorian summerhouse for family and friends by the River Trent. There were courses for employee enrichment available there, as well as sports such as tennis, grass bowls, pot-holing or canoeing, and Doreen decided to learn shorthand and typing, to give herself more skills. However, in the back of her mind, the whole time, she was thinking about her dream of being a nurse. It was still something she really wanted to find a way to do; Doreen's watchword was always,

'Where there's a will, there's a way' – she just had to find that way.

6

Seaside Sweetheart

Now Doreen was working, she was eligible to go on her first paid summer holiday, which seemed a complete and utter luxury to her. When she was younger, her family had managed to have the odd day out, or even a week, at Great Yarmouth, Skegness or Mablethorpe, but seldom could they afford more than a few days in a simple caravan or bed and breakfast. In fact, Doreen had been on more holidays with her sister Marjorie and her family than with her own, as Marjorie often had taken Doreen under her wing – plus she got free childcare into the bargain!

One summer's day, during her first year of work, Doreen, Margaret and Sylvia set off for the Lincolnshire coast together by train. The sun was shining, and Doreen felt very excited as this was her first proper outing as a real working woman. Doreen loved photographs and had scraped together enough money to get a little Brownie camera, very popular at the time, with her discount from Boots.

Mablethorpe offered pubs, fish and chips, cafés, ice-cream parlours, beach-side entertainment, such as

Punch and Judy shows in little tents, and games like quoits and crazy golf. There were bands and dances, too, at various venues.

In those days, when working people were unleashed from the daily grind and went on holiday, they headed straight for the pub to let their hair down. Indeed, both Margaret and Sylvia fancied an ale once they got to the seaside, but Doreen had developed almost a phobia about the demon drink. She didn't like it, or what it did to people. Deep inside she was a God-fearing girl, with a teetotal Methodist character just like her dear mother, and she avoided pubs like the plague. She'd seen for herself how pubs were places that changed people's characters for the worse. Doreen's experience of dealing with her dad's drunkenness and abuse, and having to go into the Railway Arms in search of him, had made her wish with all her heart that all pubs would simply burn down. It was hard for her to be moderate about it.

She explained what she could to the girls and they compromised, spending some time in the pub (with Doreen having a soft drink), and then some time in local cafés, drinking tea, or sitting on the lovely sandy beach in stripy deck chairs, having ice creams and sodas.

One afternoon, all three were sitting on the promenade, licking their ices, when a gang of boys passed by and wolf-whistled at them. Doreen's reaction was to tense up and get ready to fight, whereas the Margaret and Sylvia were quite happy to flirt.

'Ayup,' said Sylvia coquettishly to one of the gang, a handsome young man of about twenty years old – her age. He was dressed like a beatnik, with a long jumper, longish hair, big black glasses and turned-up denim jeans. Margaret started chatting to a well-dressed lad with ginger hair, but Doreen simply wanted to run away and hide. She went and sat on the sea wall and finished her ice cream, ignoring the group. The third lad in the group was shyer, with dark hair slicked back, sporting a black leather jacket and jeans. He hung back from the group for a while and watched Doreen with interest. Doreen almost buried herself in her ice cream, trying to pretend it all wasn't happening. Her two friends were chatting away very animatedly to their new-found beaus, but Doreen was panicking. What should she do next? Should she go back to their digs, or hang around and see what would happen? It was a nice sunny afternoon, so she didn't really want to be inside.

Eventually, the shy boy made his way over to where Doreen was sitting on the sea wall. He sat down next to her for a couple of minutes, wondering what to say. 'Enjoying yersel'?' he asked, tentatively.

Doreen, was now licking her fingers like a cat and trying to ignore him. Perhaps he'd go away if she didn't answer.

'Ahm Phil,' the lad tried again.

Doreen said nothing for a minute. How was she going to get out of this situation? She really didn't want to be hanging around with a boy she didn't know. Doreen just wanted to sit and look at the sea and enjoy the sun and the freedom.

'Yer from Nottingham?' asked Phil, still trying to evoke some response.

Doreen decided to look at him, finally, and when she did, she decided that he actually looked fairly harmless. In fact, he was quite good-looking, so she had no idea why he was talking to her. 'Ah am. What about yer?'

'Ahm from Leicester.'

Doreen had never been to Leicester, which was about half an hour from Nottingham by train, but could have been on the moon to her, so the conversation faltered. They sat in silence, and watched the masses of people sitting in deckchairs smoking and laughing, with knotted handkerchiefs on their heads but getting red and blistered anyway. They watched children running, shouting, skipping, playing bat and ball. Then a brass band started up on the nearby pier, playing 'Oh, I Do Like to Be Beside the Seaside'.

'Oh, I love this one,' said Doreen, forgetting her caution.

Phil laughed, and Doreen could see he had a nice, friendly face and she relaxed a bit more. They fell into conversation, which turned quickly to their respective families. Doreen was amazed to hear about Phil's extraordinary upbringing, which paralleled her own but seemed even worse.

'Ah was brought up in kids 'ome and foster care,' he explained, as the brass band played on.

'Was yer?' said Doreen, amazed. 'What were that like?'

'It were terrible,' said Phil, with feeling.

He told Doreen about how his mother had abandoned her four children when he was small, which meant they were all sent to different homes when his father died on the beach during the D-Day landings. So he lost everything and everyone, all at once. Phil had lost touch with all his siblings when he was placed into an appalling children's home. He was then fostered by people who weren't very loving or kind. Doreen felt her heart going out to the young man beside her, who had clearly had an incredibly tough life. Did she have anything to complain about with her father, after all?

Phil explained that his real mother had eventually remarried, but when she did, she had refused to take her own children back. At the time, Phil hoped they would all end up being one happy family. 'Ah would write and say "can ah come an' see yer, can ah stay?" But she always said she was "busy" or didn't have the room.'

In fact, his mother had two more children with her new husband, Phil's supposed stepfather. She just didn't want to have her first children home again as a complete family for some reason, which Phil never understood. It was if she had ditched that first part of her life, with all her responsibilities, and had simply started again.

Phil was devastated by the rejection. If he did visit, his mother would send him out to do jobs, such as chopping wood for neighbours for money, and then she'd take it off him. 'She saw me as a servant, like I was a money-making machine,' he explained to Doreen, bitterly, that sunny afternoon. 'She had lots of bedrooms, and she could have had us back all together, two in a room.' Phil was angry and upset, as he poured out his heart.

As they sat on the sandy beach, with the sun on their faces and the warm breeze blowing, Doreen felt for Phil. It was awful to lose his dad and then be rejected in such a callous way by his mum. It was terrible he'd lost his brothers and sisters, too. She loved her siblings, even the ones that drove her mad, like the beastly Jack, so her heart began to open. Here was a lovely-looking lad who had had an even worse upbringing than her own, if it was possible. It made her realise that even people who looked 'normal' on the outside often had a heart-rending story to tell.

As they sat, Phil reached over and took her hand in his. Doreen was frightened at first. Dating and boys was a whole area of life that was alien to her. But she liked Phil and, that afternoon, she let him hold her hand as they sat exchanging their stories and sharing their pain from their abusive childhoods. Funny how it was easier to talk to a stranger, Doreen thought.

After the sun set over the sea, the gang of six then went off for fish and chips and beer. Doreen and Phil carried on talking and let the other two couples go off to the pub and the penny arcades. Doreen liked the fact that Phil respected her hatred of the pub, even though he drank beer (at seventeen, he was underage, as young people couldn't drink legally until twenty-one). However, at the end of the evening when Phil leaned in for a kiss, Doreen froze. She was completely ignorant about sex and had avoided all contact with boys until now.

As was usual for the time, Doreen had had no formal sex education, and her parents had certainly never informed her about the 'facts of life', as they were called, so the area of physical intimacy was a complete mystery to her. She believed she could get pregnant from kissing, or even just touching a boy, so she was not that keen to get too close, given her experience of being the youngest in a big family. Having babies seemed to be something that had brought more strife, grief and poverty than happiness in her experience, so she wanted to avoid it at all cost.

Phil was keen, however. He liked Doreen. She was cute and feisty and different. She also listened to him and was very warm and empathic about his history. He'd never poured his heart out so quickly before, and seldom talked about his past. There was something lovely about Doreen, and for the rest of the holiday the pair spent most days together, just talking and enjoying crazy golf and eating chips and ice cream. They went to the fun fair and talked about their dreams and desires. Phil also revealed that he'd been in a bit of trouble with the law from time to time, as he'd fallen in with some bad lads, but had now straightened himself out.

Doreen warmed to him, and thought secretly that she was even falling for him. She could see he was a good lad, that he'd had a rough time and part of her wanted to help him straighten out further, even though she was scared of getting close.

'Ah've been easily led, sometimes,' confessed Phil, honestly. 'But ah want to mek something of mesel'.'

Doreen understood those words, as she wanted to make something of herself too. Perhaps they could make something of themselves together?

7

Born to Nurse

From that holiday on, the pair were going out. They soon fell deeply in love, but Doreen was terrified of letting anything physical happen between them. She allowed him a kiss and a cuddle, but that was all. She made Phil wait; she was determined that they would make something of their lives and that meant she did not want an unwanted pregnancy. She still had untutored ideas about sex – she even believed that she could get pregnant by sitting on the same toilet seat after Phil had used it.

Doreen and Phil decided to get married and set a date, some three years' hence, and both started saving. Phil worked as a delivery driver in Leicester, and they talked about him getting a better job, as his wages weren't great. Doreen, however, set out her stall to Phil from the start. 'I'm not going to marry a drinker,' she told him firmly. 'So don't marry me if you're going to be a drinker.'

Phil did like a drink at that time, and had been drunk quite often. He had to think about it. He had been off the rails due to drinking too much when he felt lonely and angry, which was when he had got into trouble with the law. 'Listen, ah love yer Doreen,' he said, sweetly. 'And fer yer, ahm only going ter have a couple from now on. Ah promise.'

Phil meant it, as the absence of family had been so excruciatingly painful to him that he wanted to keep all of sweet Doreen for himself. He didn't want to lose her. This meant he could get very jealous and possessive if she spoke to other men, and could be controlling at times, but Doreen loved him, as she could see the good in him, and she understood how badly he'd been hurt and rejected. She wanted to help him get his life on track, and she needed him to do that if he wanted to be with her – she was fed up of chaos and drama. Doreen could see potential in Phil and he could see potential in her, so they made a pact to give life a go, together.

Doreen branched out, as she loved cooking, so she joined the Territorial Army and in her spare time learned how to be their local branch cook. As the couple planned their small wedding, Doreen prepared to leave Boots, as she had to, once married. Ultimately, she was not sad to say goodbye to the warehouse job at nineteen, although she was very sad to leave Margaret and Sylvia.

'How about we mek a real effort to stay friends?' suggested Doreen, who really adored the two.

'Ahm up for it,' said Margaret.

'Me too,' said Sylvia, and not only did they stay friends during their working lives, but indeed they stayed in touch for the rest of their lives.

Meanwhile, Doreen still had not let go of her nursing dream, and it was tugging at her even more. One day, when she was still a newlywed, she saw in the *Nottingham Post* that there was a free course being put on by the British Red Cross for people who wanted to become 'first aiders'. Doreen leapt at the chance. She had always wanted to do any kind of medical training, but it was the cost that had put her off (plus the lack of encouragement). Now the Red Cross was offering to train people up for free – how could she resist? What a wonderful place to start. Doreen felt it was a marvellous opportunity, so she applied, got an interview, and, to her amazement and delight, was accepted onto the course with open arms.

Doreen knew from the start of her marriage to Phil that she didn't want a big family like the one she had come from. Doreen had seen first hand how tied down women were if they had too many mouths to feed, and too little cash and personal freedom. The spectre of her own childhood poverty and the violence of her father was never far from her mind. She was determined on two main fronts. First, to have just one child to make things affordable and manageable, unlike her poor mother, whom she had seen struggling with pregnancy after pregnancy; second, to find a way to train as a nurse, as it still remained her passion.

While Phil worked for an engineering firm as a driver, and the couple moved into a rented flat in St Ann's, Doreen continued to work for the Territorial Army as a cook. Her free Red Cross first-aid training had been successful, and she continued training with them in the evenings, and passed more courses. Soon, Doreen was asked if she would like to start running a group in Carlton, and was trained to teach first aid to all sorts of different groups. She was over the moon, as she was finally gaining medical knowledge. Meanwhile, she also got a daytime job in a supermarket, Mace, as she needed to make regular money. Liking people and being a bundle of energy meant she was happy to multi-task and do several jobs at once.

When Doreen had her son, Paul, she stayed at home for a while, but soon was itching to get back to nursing work in some way or another. She managed the home, their baby and went to work in the evenings, getting a job at Mudthorpe Nursing Home, where she gained invaluable experience. She did a stint at a home for 'subnormal children', as they were then called, in Mapperley, which was like a hospital for children with extreme developmental difficulties. She also became a school nurse and a nursing assistant some time later, receiving training as she worked. Doreen was like a medical magpie, picking up training and learning from every job she went to, always thirsting for more knowledge and experience. She became an auxiliary at Sherwood Hospital, where she was trained to give bed baths (she always liked to cover up their 'private bits' for modesty's sake), and deal with people of all ages going through all sorts of illnesses, treatments and operations. She was still an avid churchgoer, and her religious belief was an important part of her motivation to help people.

Doreen gained a lot of experience as a community auxiliary nurse, visiting the elderly in their homes and helping new mothers and their children. She also worked on the gynaecological and obstetrics ward at Nottingham Women's Hospital – 'Peel Street' – and even did a two-year stint at Queen's Medical Centre in Nottingham.

Doreen nearly always worked nights to fit round family life, which meant she and Phil had to have a really strong, working relationship. Phil had experienced a great deal of emotional fallout from his own upbringing, and Doreen's strength and determination helped him to overcome his own personal difficulties. She tried to provide Phil – and of course their son Paul – with a secure, safe environment, where they felt loved, nurtured and valued.

Despite her own mistreatment at her father's hands, and seeing his violence towards her mother and other family members, Doreen put her new nursing knowledge and skills to good use once her own father's health began to deteriorate.

In his latter years her father was not a happy man, despite forty-six years of successful train driving and the gold retirement watch he had to prove it. His lifetime of drinking had taken its toll on his body and mind, not to mention his spirit. Doreen had already lost her mother to heart failure, gangrene and pneumonia, and was heartbroken. However, her father was to have a more long-drawn out illness brought on by his hard drinking.

Despite everything, Doreen and Phil took her father in, and she nursed him through the last two years of his life. He was mentally very unstable by then, and would cut himself out of photographs and slump into depression. When he drank too much, he would say woefully the next day, 'Oh, I'm never going to drink again,' and Doreen would answer, 'Dad, let's tek all the booze away, shall we?' But, by the next night, he would be drinking again.

Doreen would come off night duty, and Phil would have got Paul up for school. Doreen would take Paul to school as Phil went off to work, and then she would attend to her collapsed father. She would give him a bath, and make him breakfast, just like tending another child.

By then, Doreen had been able to forgive him, or at least she could see that he was suffering emotionally and mentally as well as physically, even if his condition was down to his bad habits. She was able to see he was unhappy due to his own childhood with his weird and frightening mother, and found she could feel sorry for him, despite all his own wrong-doings. Due to her faith, it was important for Doreen to strive to understand her father and approach him with some genuine compassion. She didn't ever really feel comfortable with him, but she realised that, deep down, she did care for him, and that he deserved some humane treatment in his hour of need.

Doreen was with him when he died, as he vomited blood and his body gave out. Later, Doreen would perform a similar task with her older brother, Jack, who despised her and was a difficult person to the end. It wasn't that Doreen was a saint, it was that, despite everything, she found that actually loved her flesh and blood. What's more, she wanted to do what she felt was the right thing, and in doing so she could live with herself, in peace.

Doreen has spent the rest of her life caught up in caring and nursing, and taking good care of her family. She remains very health-conscious, perhaps due to having experienced a lot of ill health and continued asthma from childhood. She is positive, outgoing and a real force to be reckoned with regarding local campaigns and community. She has researched her family history and is a keen local historian. True to her own history, she is very concerned about the amount of alcohol that people are drinking today.

Doreen remains a good woman, with a giving heart, who still lives by the Methodist principles her mother instilled in her. She retired at sixty, but will continue to be feisty, optimistic and caring to the last.

Bob Cox

Vintage magazine illustration.

1

Biker's Dream

'Ayup, Bob.'

'Ayup, Mr Unwin.'

Ten-year-old Bob Cox was standing next to the most wonderful object he had ever seen: a beautiful black and chrome Triumph Tiger 100 motorcycle that gleamed in the sun.

Mr Unwin, Bob's neighbour and the owner of the bike, was a squat ex-military man with bulging biceps inked with serpentine tattoos and hearts. His chest flexed under his smudged white vest, and he wore black trousers and braces with shiny black Dr Marten boots and a flat cap. As Bob ogled the beautiful new machine with pure wonder, Mr Unwin smeared some Duraglit onto a rag and polished the chrome until it sparkled. Mr Unwin always had a roll-up stuck in the corner of his mouth, with a curve of grey ash hanging off it and smoke curling constantly upwards in the warm summer evening. 'Want ter help?'

He threw him a yellow duster and Bob eagerly got down on his bare knees on the kerb, and started rubbing the metal for all his life was worth.

'Ah'll tek yer fer a spin, if yer like?' said Mr Unwin, puffing on his ciggie, his eyes squinting with effort.

Ash fell on the pavement and Bob rubbed the bike all the harder, 'That'll be grand.'

Bob's heart was bursting with excitement, and as Mr Unwin tightened and adjusted screws and nuts, Bob rubbed the chrome till it gleamed. He fell in love with the wondrous, speedy beast and vowed he'd have one himself when he was grown up, one day.

In 1955, Bob lived at the top end of Schooner Street in Radford, just west of Nottingham city centre. Radford was one of the most downtrodden areas of Nottingham, an urban area created by the overspill from the city centre during the rapid industrial expansion of the nineteenth and twentieth centuries. The ailing and waning Churchill, a magnificent leader during the Second World War, resigned in April of that year as prime minister and was replaced by Anthony Eden, signalling a new, quieter era in British politics. Rationing had ended the previous year, but life still felt tough, even though things were getting back to some kind of normality and standards were very gradually improving, not least within health and education. The National Health Service had been born in 1948, and the school leaving age had been raised to fourteen.

Radford was an overcrowded place filled with endless roads of red-brick tenements along the River Leen. It was heavily industrialised, with cotton and worsted mills, bleach works, bobbin net mills, lace makers and a pit. Its dense overpopulation meant it was full of pubs, clubs, chapels, churches, shops, services and a vibrant local farmers' and craftsmen's market on Saturdays.

Bob's parents, Sidney and Rosie, had started their married life in a dingy flat in a two-up-two-down in St Ann's, a notoriously rough district, even more impoverished than Radford. When the opportunity arose to 'move up' in the world, they moved to Radford when Rosie was pregnant with Bob, as they thought they would need help from Rosie's mother, who lived there already.

Sidney worked at the Raleigh in the aptly named Triumph Road in Nottingham as a plumber, as did his brother Arnold. His sister Mavis worked there too, in the toy department, while Rosie packed cigarettes at the Players cigarette factory on Player Street in Radford. She gave up when Bob came along, but went back later.

Although their house in Radford was a step up from the flat in St Ann's, it was still fairly basic: the red bricks were black from soot, it had no heating or running water except an outside tap in the backyard, and there was only a primitive outside 'lavvy'. There were no power sockets, only one light bulb in each room and any heating was from coal, which had to be delivered by the local coalman who brought it round on carts or in a truck. Bob's job was to fold old newspapers into paper 'chickens' to start the fire. Their house was at the bottom of a long row of about forty on Schooner Street: typically, it was freezing in winter, and roasting in summer, but it was home.

Like many young lads, Bob was smitten by the wonders of the motorcycle, and he loved the feeling of the wind in his hair and the throb of the engine beneath him as he hung onto Mr Unwin's back for dear life. He imagined himself grown up, on his own bike, flying over distant, dusty roads, clad in leathers, with not a care in the world.

At that time there were only a few cars in Radford, generally a Ford or an Austin and usually black in colour, and they were too expensive for ordinary working people to run. The roads were full of walkers and bicycles, mothers with prams, children with hoops and balls. Mr Unwin's Triumph bike fed Bob's fantasies wonderfully. As an only child he was a bit of a loner, although he had a couple of good mates on the street, a couple of close schoolfriends and plenty of cousins.

Socially, Sidney and Rosie spent most time with their family, friends and neighbours, and many Saturday nights they'd pop down the road to Granny's house and get a jug or two of ale in from the local beer off. The whole family sat in Granny's tiny downstairs room, or in the summer out the front on kitchen chairs, and talked shop, politics or family matters.

Bob, a quiet, intense boy, usually had something with him to take apart: an old wireless, a torch or a broken watch to fix. Bob also loved making Airfix kits. While the adults chatted over their beer and fags, Bob would be given a Vimto or an Irn-Bru to drink. He often heard his father say, 'It's not what yer know, but who yer know,' as the adults spoke endlessly, sometimes arguing, about rates of pay, jobs going, unions, hours of work. They supped the ale from Home Brewery and ate homemade sausage rolls, as they put the world to rights.

'There were over a hundred at the gate,' Sidney would say, describing the usual weekly jobs queue outside the Raleigh on a Monday morning. As a matter of course, over a hundred workers would be laid off on a Friday, only for the same number or more to be hired again on a Monday.

'We 'ad a 'undred an' fifty at ours,' chipped in Rosie, 'An' still counting.'

Workers would ask around or chat on street corners, in pubs and shops, to find out who was hiring, or who paid the best. They constantly wanted to 'up' their wages by moving around from factory to factory.

'Reckon ahm stayin' put,' Sidney would say decisively, taking a slug of his beer. 'Ah don't mind Raleigh's, ah can bear the work.'

In fact, he was immensely proud of his work as a plumber, and Bob could see that his father liked belonging to such a well-established firm with a good manufacturing reputation worldwide. Despite the long hours and noisy, dirty workshops, Sidney would say, over his beer, 'It could be worse, son. We've lived through't war, so we know it can always get worse.'

2

The Milk Bar Kid

Bob went to the local infant and primary in Radford, and then on to the secondary modern. He wasn't particularly academic or bookish, but he did enjoy the metalwork and woodwork classes. He loved using his hands, and found it amazing how you could take a lump of wood and gradually chip off the bark and shape it into something like a stool leg or a fruit bowl.

Bob liked music, and sang in the school choir, and began to creep into milk bars or coffee bars in Radford, where they had a magical thing called a jukebox. Bob loved slipping a sixpence into the Wurlitzer and pressing the buttons for his favourite popular hits: Bill Haley's 'Rock Around the Clock', Elvis Presley's 'All Shook Up' and Pat Boone's 'Love Letters in the Sand'. Bob was one of the new social breed named 'teenagers', and he and his friends would sit for hours over a frothy coffee in glass cups and saucers, or drink flavoured milkshakes or bottles of Coca-Cola. It was a great place for shy Bob to meet girls.

Life at home was fairly quiet, with his mother doing the

washing on a Monday, cooking tea every night, while his father tinkered with the Hoover when it needed mending or fixed a dripping tap when it leaked. Bob loved it when the chimney sweep came to clean the chimney, a filthy job that had to be done once a year, at least. He would come with a barrow, and later with a little Austin van, loaded up with black brushes and bags, and Bob's mother would cover the living room floor with dust sheets and old newspapers. The sweep then approached the fire grates – there was one downstairs and one upstairs in Bob's parents' bedroom – and sealed the fireplace off with special sheeting with a hole in the middle of it. He then got a series of poles and screwed them together, one at a time, with a big round brush on the end, which he pushed slowly and deftly up the chimney, using a kind of screwing motion. As the rods with the brush went up the chimney, the soot loosened and started falling down, where it was caught at the bottom in the sheeting. Bob and his mates would stand outside of the house and wait for the brush to pop out of the chimney – it was always a sight that made them laugh and cheer. Then the brush was brought down the chimney, one rod at a time, as each length was unscrewed and dismantled, until the brush end was back on the floor again.

The sweep tried to make sure all the loosened soot ended up in the sacks, but there was always a lot of it scattered around the grate and the living room, as it was very difficult to get all of it. Sometimes the sweep left one sack behind, and Sidney took the contents and dug them into his plot at the local allotment, for its nourishing mineral content. There was always a lot of clearing up to do afterwards and Bob's mother would moan about the mess, but it was 'all hands on deck', swabbing the floor. In actual fact, Bob found it great fun as he liked being practical.

By the time Bob was thirteen, there was a lot of talk round the tea table, and at his Granny's on Saturday nights, about what he should do when he left school. Money was tight, and it was made clear, at school and at home, that he would be leaving at fourteen, just like most of his friends. Few people from Bob's community went to university, it was something that was out of the league of ordinary people at that time, and it never crossed Bob's mind to think about it at all.

His father started a campaign for Bob to become a plumber like himself, it was his Raleigh-ing call. 'Look at yer aunt and uncle, look at me, we're not complaining,' Sidney argued over their fish and chip supper.

Bob was not convinced as his father complained constantly about the working conditions, the long hours, management, the shift work and tricky jobs. He had a bit of a love–hate relationship with the Raleigh. Bob also heard his friends at school talking about better pay down the pits, often three times as good.

'Even Players paid better than the Raleigh,' or so his mother would say sometimes, to settle an argument.

'Look, son,' his father would begin, trying hard to be patient, 'yer want to learn a trade, a proper job, summat to lean on – an' yer good wi' yer 'ands.'

What was clear to Bob was that his schooling was coming to an end, and he'd have to pay his way. His father was pushing him into the 'family business', in other words, the Raleigh – and it felt to Bob he didn't really have a say in the matter.

3

The Raleigh-ing Call

'Name?' The uniformed man at the gate was looking at his clipboard.

'Robert Cox,' said Bob shyly.

The man looked down the list. 'Ah, yes. Go through to reception,' he said, and ticked off Bob's name with a pencil attached to the board by string.

Bob sat, in his best school blazer and shorts, and felt very nervous. The building was enormous. He had visited his dad's giant workshop a few times, but his heart was racing thinking that he might actually work there himself.

Raleigh had originally started in central Nottingham in Raleigh Street in 1885. Bicycling became fashionable and popular as a cheap mode of transport. At first it was deemed unseemly for women, but it was extremely popular for both sexes by the mid-twentieth century. The exponential growth in bike sales not only in Britain, but worldwide, meant it soon outgrew its premises. In 1922, thirty-one enormous purpose-built Deco-style buildings were erected on Lenton Boulevard, which included a theatre, a ballroom, dining rooms and show rooms. It was all part of the paternalistic culture that developed in manufacturers who had a social conscience. The Raleigh was known locally and nationally to be a good employer.

Bob sat in an oak-lined boardroom on a chair and felt sick. He was facing a series of desks curved round the room in a horseshoe, with nine managers and directors, all in dark suits and ties, firing questions at him. As Bob sat there, mumbling his way through the barrage the best he could, he realised he didn't know exactly what plumbing entailed, despite his father explaining it to him many times. His mind went back to the night before, when Sidney had come home and thrown his canvas bag on the kitchen floor with a rattlely clunk.

'Tek a little look at this lot, son,' he'd said gruffly.

Bob knew his tools were his father's pride and joy, and usually he wasn't allowed to touch them. He'd felt honoured, and had opened the bag and picked up a big, greasy wrench. It was surprisingly heavy. Then he'd handled a metal hammer and some weird wire-cutting objects.

'Tools of the trade, lad,' said Sidney. 'Used them, man and boy, for forty year at Raleigh. Some of them were my fathers, even my grandfather's.' He took out a pair of pliers. 'Cop a feel of these, son.'

Bob handled the tool, turning it over, and weighed it in his square hands.

'Reckon yer should look through this little lot, familiarise yersel' with them. I can explain more to yer, if yer like, tomorra.'

Bringing his thoughts back to the interview, Bob sorely wished he'd listened closer, as he was not sure he was answering the questions properly. 'So Robert, tell us why you want to learn about plumbing?' said a Mr Hanson in a thick navy pinstriped suit with glasses.

Bob cleared his throat, and took a deep breath.

Later, on the bus home, he wasn't sure he'd answered correctly. He'd found himself talking about his father and grandfather, and feeling almost like he was part of the firm already. Bob thought it was probably the wrong thing to say. Anyway, he wasn't convinced he wanted an apprenticeship for six whole years because of the low wages. There had been arguments at home recently, as his mother was annoyed he was doubting Raleigh.

Once home, he told her honestly that he felt despondent about his chances of success.

'Well, that's it,' she said, hands on hips. 'Yer not sitting 'ere, moping about. If yer think yer are, yer can think again. You'll go out and get a job, and you'll earn some money. You'll not sit round here under my feet and that's for sure.'

Rosie explained that no son of hers was going on a production line, either. 'Yer going to learn a proper trade, an' get a proper job, not just do some dead-end job on a conveyor belt.'

Good to her word, the next week Rosie told Bob that he was to turn up the next Monday at a plumber's yard in Lenton. He was to take the job, as they hadn't heard from Raleigh's, and no arguing back.

The following Monday, he started at Roper's, off Willoughby Street, and began to go on call outs with the large, rambling Mr Biggs, who had been a plumber all his life. Bob quite enjoyed holding the spanner for him as he sorted out a U-bend, or doing a bit of welding back at the workshop. He began to enjoy the discipline of getting up and going on the bus to Lenton, and couple of weeks into working at Roper's he thought it wasn't too bad at all. He enjoyed the pipework, and he liked the lads, even if he did get ribbed a lot as a new boy. He thought he could be a real plumber, no problem. He enjoyed being with the men, especially going to the Plumber's Arms at lunchtime, and learning to drink a pint of Kimberley Ale to accompany his crusty cheese cob.

At the end of his third week he arrived home around six in the evening and gave his meagre wages to his mother. 'There's a letter,' she said, briskly.

A manila envelope was propped up on the mantelpiece clock. Bob never got letters, not ones specifically addressed to him, and he went over and picked it up, turning it over with his grubby hands, leaving finger marks. It was all very official-looking.

'Go on, aren't yer going ter open it?'

Bob ripped it open and found, to his amazement, that Raleigh was offering him an apprenticeship after all.

'Well, they took their time,' his mother said.

Bob knew it was her way of saying she was pleased. She went to the stove and put on the kettle, lighting a match. Bob felt strangely elated. 'You are offered an Apprenticeship in Plumbing,' it said. Now it was real, he felt really excited, especially as he'd already enjoyed his three weeks working at Roper's. Indeed, this letter did seem to suggest something more solid, more official, and with more scope. But he was also scared to commit himself to a six-year haul – six years seemed like a life-time. He'd be twenty-one when he finished. An adult. Grown up.

Rosie sat down at the table, wiping her hands on a tea towel. 'Aren't yer pleased, lad? Yer've done well. Yer dad'll be so proud.'

Bob thought for a moment, 'Ah know, ah am … it's just that a lot of me friends are already getting double this.' He was looking at the terms on the bottom of the letter.

'Ah see,' his mother said, sounding somewhat exasperated, 'Look, son, it's a big firm. Yer'll be trained properly, yer'll probably get day release fer yer City and Guilds.'

Bob realised would take years for him to save for that dream motorbike, all gleaming chrome, swanky dials and big tyres. For a moment he saw himself hurtling across the Mohave Desert on his throbbing beast ... how long would it take to get one, he wondered?

'Yer won't regret it, son,' his mother continued her campaign. 'Look at yer dad now, he's head of his department.'

There were over four hundred maintenance men at the Raleigh, and his dad was always telling them at home about his call outs and jobs, so the work sounded varied enough. It was his little plumbing fiefdom. Bob looked at his mother's face, which implored him to see sense.

'OK, ah'll put in me notice tomorra,' he said, slowly, and watched her face relax visibly. 'Ah'll tek the apprenticeship. Ah really do want to mek you both proud.'

4

Tooling Up for the Job

Bob soon discovered there was a lot to learn about plumbing. When he started his apprenticeship at the Raleigh, the company employed about 7,500 people in Nottingham spread out over several locations: a huge main factory at Lenton and one on Castle Boulevard, called the Pressworks, both of which made bicycles; plus a pram factory at Bramcote. Outside Nottingham, there was a specialist racing cycle factory, called Carlton Cycles, at Worksop.

On Bob's first day in Nottingham, Barny, the foreman, a stout man in his fifties in faded blue overalls, took Bob to one side and explained the importance of time keeping. 'Yer can tell the time, can't yer lad?' he asked sardonically.

Bob didn't know whether to laugh or not, so he nodded, serious-faced, as he wanted to please his new boss. They were standing by a huge metal clock contraption on the wall, near the staff entrance, with a battery of cards in slots ready to be stamped.

'Yer to be 'ere seven thirty and no later – that's when yer clock in,' Barny explained gruffly, picking up a beige card and putting it in a slot in the machine and punching a button, which made it ting. 'If yer not 'ere by seven thirty, yer 'ave to wait till quarter to. Frank, in security, will check whether yer wanted or not that day. Got it?'

Bob nodded again, but wasn't entirely clear. 'So, what happens if I'm late?'

Barny's face hardened, 'If yer not 'ere by half past, you only have one more chance … at a quarter to we'll decide if yer wanted or not. If not, yer'll be sent 'ome without pay if yer're even a minute late,' he said.

Bob could tell he wasn't joking and he didn't fancy testing him. It was clearly a strict regime, and explained a lot about his father.

What lay ahead was six years of low pay and training. On the one hand, Bob was pleased as he had secured the proper apprenticeship in engineering his mother had wanted him to get, but on the other, he was still peeved as his mates were boasting about how much they earnt, and they were able to buy more pints and records at the weekend. However, the work was really quite interesting. Bob found himself fascinated by anything to do with pipes, water, steam, and gases: he really like the pipefitting as he found it satisfying work.

Bob's dad's friend also worked at Raleigh as a toolsetter and one break time he went and found him. He watched as he set his tools by winding a huge crank, on a large flywheel, until it hit a piece of metal on his workbench, with a loud 'ka-junk', and punched out a shaped tool. He could create a tool out of a piece of steel to a thousandth of an inch. Bob was utterly impressed.

Bob was also amazed at the range of skills that were being used at the Raleigh. There were upholsterers, blacksmiths and all sorts. He went and watched Eric, an upholsterer, and learned how to cover a chair (Raleigh did their own office refurbishments then). Later, Bob was able to cover chairs at home, which pleased his mother. There was a furnace for metal work, and he loved watching the blacksmith beat out tools as he hammered white hot metal into shape on the anvil. There was also a joinery, and Bob was fascinated to watch objects emerge from the lathe.

At first, Bob's job was simply to watch the men in his own giant workshop, which was deafeningly noisy. Then he started at Nottingham Technical College to do his City and Guilds course. Luckily for Bob, they had just streamlined the system, so instead of having to go to college for one day a week for six years, he could do 'block release', which meant studying for a whole week at a time, once or twice a term, plus three nights a week. Bob was really pleased and relieved that he'd be able to complete his apprenticeship in almost half the time. Nonetheless, he was still annoyed about the money, as that gleaming motorbike was still in the forefront of his mind's eye.

One Friday, a year into his training and now sixteen, Bob was about to hand over his wages to his mother, as usual, when he paused. 'Ah want a pair of shoes,' he said, 'So can ah keep some back?' Bob was gradually turning into a bit of a rocker and there was a pair of biker boots in town he was lusting after.

'We can't afford it,' snapped Rosie. 'Think on.'

Bob was riled. 'You've had all my money all this time. It's not fair.'

'Ah'll gi' yer not fair,' said his mother, about to clock him with the back of her hand.

Rosie had a temper on her, and had a habit of picking up one of her shoes and hitting people she disagreed with over the head. He had seen her do it with the pointed heel of a stiletto before now, and Bob was wary of pushing her too far. 'But Mother—' Bob started.

'Ah'll "but mother" yer …' she said. 'If yer can afford shoes, yer can afford to pay me more.'

And indeed that was the outcome, as Bob's contribution to the household was increased. His mother had worked in a ball-bearing factory, Ransom and Marles, in Newark, before she married, but now she worked at Players as well as running the house. It was a solid matriarchy. Nonetheless, Bob managed to salt away what he could, as that vision of the bike purring at the kerbside was what really kept him going through the long days learning to fit pipes and, at college, learning from his lectures and books.

Unusually for the era, Bob was an only child. His mother been 'in the family way' when his parents married in 1947, which was extremely socially shameful at the time. There was another pregnancy but Rosie sadly miscarried. Both his parents came from large families and, after the struggle of the war years, decided they wanted to keep their family small. This meant Bob felt a lot of pressure on him to please both his parents, as there were no other siblings to hide behind or to deflect the parental gaze. Sometimes the pressure got too much, which made Bob a bit rebellious, even secretive. He had to protect his privacy and individuality some way – especially as the whole family seemed to be working at the Raleigh and both his grannies lived in Radford.

Being in the apprenticeship fast lane meant he worked hard, trained hard and studied hard, which pleased Bob no end, as it halved the time it would take for him to become qualified. Indeed, by the time he was seventeen, he had succeeded in becoming a fully qualified plumber. Bob was immensely pleased to be moved on to proper working man's wages. As part of his training he had to do a stint working in all the different departments at the Raleigh. He would arrive at work (on time, of course), and go through to the plumbing department. A secretary would come through and hand a job card to Barny the supervisor. Barny would then hand it out to the appropriate plumber, who would be sent off to sort out the job.

Once Bob became qualified, the secretary, Marsha, would say, 'Ayup, Bob, job fer yer,' and hand him a card.

'Thanks, Marsha, lass,' said Bob.

He would read the card and then find himself a mate – an apprentice or labourer – and take his bag of tools to the relevant department. By the end of the day, the job card would be handed to Marsha with a proud, 'Job done.' The more jobs he cleared, the better his pay at the end of the week, as there was a 'piecework' scheme in place, as there was in most factories at that time.

5

Getting Back on the Bike

'Come on, Bob, we're going out.' Bob's best friend from work, Jim, was standing on his doorstep.

'Nah, don't feel like it.'

'Come on, ah'll not tek no fer an answer,' said Jim, coming into the hall, and picking Bob's black leather biker jacket off the hook on the wall. 'Yer need to get out. It's Christmas.'

Bob knew there was no convincing Jim once he'd made up his mind, and so they headed for Nottingham on the bus. Bob was now twenty-one, and was nursing a broken heart. He'd had a whirlwind romance with Betty, one of the Raleigh secretaries, which had ended up in marriage, but the relationship hadn't worked out and he was now separated, to his chagrin. Most people felt then if you weren't married by the time you were twenty-one, you were 'on the shelf'. With his separation, Bob felt he was fully back on the shelf.

In the heady days of Bob and Betty's passionate romance, it had felt like the real thing. However, after they were married, they soon found out they were incompatible and started arguing about everything all the time. Betty was a vivacious young woman who attracted a lot of male attention, which upset Bob. He realised he had made a big mistake, so they split up, just before Christmas the year before, much to his mother's outrage. She believed – as most people did then – that you should stick with marriage, however unhappy it made you. 'Yer mek yer bed, and yer lie in it, son.'

A year on, Bob was still licking his wounds, and not wanting to go out much, despite (or even perhaps because of) it being the festive season. The lifestyle of 'the Raleigh lads' was notoriously raucous: work hard, play hard, very much as described in Nottingham-born Alan Sillitoe's *Saturday Night and Sunday Morning*. At 'dinnertime' the lads would hit a pub, like the Nag's Head, and have three pints with their crusty cobs and crisps, and chat up the girls from the local factories and shops. There was a lot of flirting, teasing, banter and sexual innuendoes in the air.

Bob had married Betty thinking he was truly in love, that it was for life, and would lead to their building a family. He felt sore that it hadn't worked out.

'Plenty more fish in the sea,' said Jim, with his usual fortitude.

'Hmmm,' said Bob, over his fourth pint of Kimberley Ale. Being rejected in love had hurt.

'Look, yer a young lad, yer can't gi' up. Yer got ter get

back on't bike, if yer see what ah mean,' Jim said, guffawing at his own joke. 'Come on, we're goin' dancin'.'

With that, Jim pulled Bob off his bar stool and they headed for the Palais de Danse, the usual Saturday night venue for dancing and courting in Nottingham. It was quite late when they got there, about ten thirty. The dance floor was packed with girls dancing away together while the lads stood round the sides of the room, nursing their pints.

Bob spied an attractive gaggle of girls across the room and, fuelled by beer, he downed his pint and said, 'Come on, then,' to Jim, and they went over and asked the girls to dance.

They both had a dance with most of the girls in the gang. Right at the end, but before the night was over, there was one girl left Bob hadn't danced with yet. She was small, with blond hair and green eyes, and had a cute face. As he turned to approach her, she let rip at him. 'Yer took yer time, what are yer doing leaving me till last?'

Bob was taken aback by her forthrightness and didn't know what to say. He hadn't really noticed her, until now. Was she angry with him or joking? The young woman broke into a warm, inviting smile, 'Come on then, ask me to dance, will yer?'

Bob grabbed her to him, and smiled, and they started moving together round the floor. 'Ahm Sandra,' she said.

'Bob,' he replied, and they danced together to the music, laughing at what had just happened.

Bob was intrigued. Sandra was quirky, and feisty, and Bob found himself attracted to someone for the first time since his split. After that dance ended, they danced to the next, and then Bob took Sandra home to where she lived in a terrace with her granny in St Ann's. On the way home, they discovered, very quickly, that they had a lot in common. Both had married too soon, and both marriages were as good as ended. When she was fifteen, Sandra had fallen into a relationship with a neighbour's son, and then they had drifted into early marriage. 'But it's become more like brother and sister really,' she explained to Bob. 'The spark is gone.'

Bob told Sandra how his heart had been broken by his wife flirting with the lads at work. He realised very soon into his marriage that he couldn't trust her, and they didn't really get on.

Bob and Sandra discovered they were both disappointed in love, and were both recovering from relationships that hadn't worked out. From that night on, they became utterly inseparable.

Soon after they met, as they sat in the pub on a freezing January night, Sandra told Bob about her own upbringing, which had been fairly tough but typical of the time. Bob had a pint and Sandra a half, as she began, 'My father worked down Clifton Pit. Apparently, it was love at first sight, and they soon married.' In fact, Sandra didn't know exactly how they met, the where or when, but imagined it would have been in a pub or at the dance hall. 'They lived in St Ann's, in a typical two-up-two-down.'

'Just like us,' interjected, Bob, 'That's where my parents started out.' They nodded and sipped their beers. They both knew the privations and the joys of the Meadows.

'Me father was a bit of a womaniser,' said Sandra, sadly, 'So by the time I was two, he had other women on the go, so me mother threw him out.'

Sandra explained that her father emigrated to Australia, hoping for a new and better life. Meanwhile, a lot of Sandra's relatives worked down the same pit, and Sandra, who had delivered papers to the pit as a child earning a shilling or two a week, remembered going to see the winding wheel, the canteen and the lamp shop, where the furnace was kept.

'Me mother remarried soon after, and I have a half-brother.'

For a while, the newly formed family was happy, and Sandra went to school and life went on. Then her granny, also living in St Ann's, quite nearby, had an accident, and had to go into hospital. Sandra was now eleven, and her mother and stepdad decided that when Granny came home, Sandra would be the one to live with Granny, to look after her as she wouldn't be mobile. 'Because I was the only girl in the family, they all decided it should be me who lived wi' her,' Sandra explained to Bob. 'For some reason it couldn't be my brother, so it had to be me.'

From then on, Sandra lived with her granny, and did her washing, shopping, cooking and got herself to school every day. Her mother, stepfather and brothers were living one street away, so at least she saw them frequently. Sandra missed a lot of school, and left at fifteen with no qualifications, so it was decided (by the school, mainly) that she would go to Players.

'We went as a big group of us from school, and they divided us up into different sections: packing, rolling, the labs, and so on. I worked in the labs, testing the moisture in the tobacco,' explained Sandra. 'I was always on my feet, walking for miles between three factories to collect samples. I had to weigh the different types of tobacco, then put them in ovens overnight, then weigh them again in the morning. This is how they knew how much the tobacco retained moisture. I had to write a little report on them, and show it to the foreman, who then checked if the tobacco was okay. It was called "quality control".' One ghoulish thing about the job was this: 'People called us "Players Angels" cos so many of the girls died so young from breathing in the tobacco dust.'

'Blimey, sounds dangerous,' said Bob, sipping his beer thoughtfully.

Sandra had the same 'letting in' time experience as Bob, in that if she was one minute late she was turned away for the day. She had two 'letting in' times: 8am and 8.15am, and, after that, she had to go home without pay. Even so, Sandra enjoyed the job, as she liked the camaraderie of working with the girls on her section, and the fact that she walked around the factory, meeting lots of new people. 'Also me mum was working in the canteen then as a dinner lady, and I'd go past her with my tray and she'd give me an extra portion of chips, wi' a wink.'

Sandra quite enjoyed the routine, getting to work for 8am and finishing at 5pm. It was regular work, for regular money, and she felt good in her heavy-duty overall, walking around with a clipboard. 'I made good friends at Players, and the job was better as I had more freedom than the girls that were just stuck on the machinery.'

Bob could understand that. 'Yes, I know what yer mean, as ah like being able to go round the Raleigh and do me different jobs. It's a sense of freedom.'

The girls got chatted up a lot, of course, as they went round the factory all day. 'We'd talk to all the electricians, and to the lads who worked on the rumblers, where the leaf came in.' Bob could relate to this, as he was used to a lot of banter and flirting, it was what oiled the wheels at work. The 'Players Angels' even got up to hijinks and took in a Ouija board, which was all the rage at the time, and tried to call up spirits in the ladies' lavatory (amid a lot of giggles). Someone would be a lookout, and then they would shout 'foreman's coming', and there would be a scramble to put the board away and pretend nothing at all was going on.

'But the pay weren't great, and ah heard on the grapevine that there were better paid machinist jobs going at Campion clothing factory, so after three years, ah left.'

It was the end of an era. Around this time, Sandra's mother got sick, and died at forty-eight after a very short illness. Sandra was distraught, and perhaps that was one of the reasons she had married her first husband so early and easily, as it was good to have someone to cling on to. But now she had met Bob, and, although she was still living with her granny and her young husband, she understood the relationship was finally over.

As they left the pub, arm in arm, Bob picked up his helmet and handed Sandra another one. Outside the pub was his pride and joy: Bob had finally managed to scrape together enough money to buy his first motorbike. He was proud of his second-hand Triumph Tiger 100. Its chrome was gleaming – Mr Unwin would have been proud of him – and he kept it in good condition as he knew how to take it apart and maintain it. Sandra wasn't that keen on bikes at first, but she knew that the way to

Bob's heart was through his motorcycle. So she put on her helmet and straddled the bike behind him, she was willing to give it a go.

6

Tandem for Life

It was time for a change. Bob and Sandra fell in love after courting for a few months, and soon decided to marry. This meant Sandra had to extricate herself from her first husband, with whom she was still living like brother and sister in St Ann's. She went to live with her auntie while going out with Bob, and her husband was devastated as, despite the marriage having died, he didn't expect Sandra would leave him for someone new.

Sandra left Campion and went to work as a machinist in a small factory on Middle Pavement in central Nottingham, just off Market Square. Meanwhile, Bob divorced his wife and continued to work at the Raleigh, where he was very settled and liked the daily variety of plumbing.

As the Raleigh had six departments, and over 400 maintenance men, there was always something new to learn, always a new challenge, which Bob enjoyed. There were annual outings to the seaside – Mablethorpe or Skegness – and the usual round of Christmas parties and birthday celebrations. Bob was proud of working in such a large and prestigious organisation, and secretly thanked his parents for having understood the importance of getting a good training.

Sandra and Bob married and moved to a little house in Beeston. Sandra worked as a machinist until Susan, their daughter, arrived, followed by John, eighteen months later. They then had two miscarriages, sadly, and decided to stop trying for a bigger family.

The family had the usual week or two of bucket and spade holidays at Great Yarmouth and Skegness, and a trip to the famous annual Goose Fair in Nottingham, which the children loved.

Outside of work, Bob's passion for bikes continued. He always had to have a motorbike of some sort, and at the weekend would forever be tinkering with it, like Mr Unwin, his first hero, mending it, cleaning it and customising it. Sandra tolerated him being such a 'grease monkey', although she wasn't that enamoured, at first.

Eventually Bob managed to find himself a second-hand BSA GoldStar, finally the real thing – which made his heart sing. This was Bob's pride and joy, his childhood passion realised, and it cost a lot of money to buy, and quite a lot to maintain. He joined the local motorbike club, and there was a little friction between him and Sandra on occasion about the amount of time and money his hobby seemed to take up. To be fair, he always spent time with his children, showing them his skills or just having fun. However, Bob had achieved his life-long dream of having his own bike and he knew he had to see it through. Sandra tended to let him go off and do his own thing, and socially would go out with her girlfriends for a drink or ice skating, or to the cinema.

One autumn evening, as Bob was leaving their house in his leathers with a spring in his step, Sandra asked him, casually, 'Where are yer going?'

'To the club, of course,' he said. 'We always meet at the pub.'

Bob was a bit perplexed as he had been going to the pub, once a week, for about six months at this time, as he loved his fellow motorbike enthusiasts. Sandra thought for a moment, 'Who'll be there?'

Bob paused, wondering whether to tell all, but thought, why not? 'Bikers, of course, and bikers' girlfriends, bikers' wives, yer know, the usual.'

'Oh, okay …' Sandra looked thoughtful as he went out the door.

The very next week, Bob was at the club in the pub and Sandra suddenly appeared, fully clad in leathers, with a helmet in her hand.

Bob's jaw dropped to the floor. 'What's going off then? We 'aven't arranged nowt, 'ave we?'

He was totally perplexed as Sandra had stubbornly refused to go to his bikers' pubs and clubs over the years, and it had become a source of some tension between them.

'Oh,' said Sandra nonchalantly, 'Ahm not 'ere fer you ... ah've come fer me lesson.'

To Bob's utter amazement (and secret admiration), Sandra rode off with a rather handsome Triumph biker clad in black leathers for her first motorcycle tuition. And to Bob's surprise and joy, Sandra passed her test with flying colours, the first time.

After this defining moment in their relationship, they rode tandem whenever they could, enjoying hurtling across the dales and whizzing through vales, feeling the wind in their faces and relishing the expansive freedom and speed. Eventually Bob even bought Sandra her own second-hand Triumph, which he maintained impeccably and with love, just so they could be a biker couple, riding off together into the industrial sunset in their matching leathers.

'If yer can't beat 'em, join 'em, that's what ah say,' explained Sandra, to a rather bemused, but happy, Bob.

7

Watching Leathers

Like his father and grandfather before him, Bob spent almost all of his working life at the Raleigh. He loved his job and enjoyed the variety of things he made and problems he solved each day. He worked at Lenton in the huge factory for over thirty years. His job was only brought to an end by the growth of cheap Chinese, Taiwanese and Korean imports, which began to challenge (and eventually destroy) the British bike market. Eventually, they became dominant and more and more Raleigh workers were laid off.

Then Bob decided to move to a small family firm. He found himself in a completely new environment, so different from the rough and tough Raleigh factory. Bob always liked working with his hands, and felt the same sort of pride in his tools as his dad had when he showed him his toolkit that day before his interview.

Retiring at sixty, Bob was able to devote his time to tinkering with his wonderful BSA, and going on road trips with his beloved Sandra (who continued as a machinist until her retirement).

Now, Bob is a devoted father and grandfather and enjoys fixing plumbing problems for the family. Sandra and Bob recently went on a motorbike road trip around the UK. As an act of devotion to the cause of the bike, they are planning trips across Europe and the Balkans, *Easy Rider*-style, in their matching leathers, very soon.

Final Thoughts

My own mother was forced to leave school at fourteen and work in Woolworth's, just post-war, despite being a bright bookish and sporty child who loved learning, and despite being told she should stay on and become a teacher. And when I met the wonderfully inspiring people in this book, it quickly became clear to me that they had all been given a similar Hobson's choice – go to work, or go to work. Boy or girl, their mission was to go out and bring home money and put it on the table. Paying their way was their number one concern in order to keep their families.

Britain in the 1930s was reeling from the economic stringencies of the First World War and was in the midst of the Depression. Nottingham, nestled in the manu-facturing heartlands of Britain, played a special role in producing what the country needed to fight and survive. Derek, Betty and Albert's families were barely recover-ing from the war and all experienced incredible grief and hardship. Each of them had to find the strength to endure and make something of themselves, which, in Derek's case, culminated in a meteoric rise to the top of Boots.

Every person, in their own way, made the very best of what they had. Pauline, Doreen and Bob were just as resourceful and determined as the elder three in teaching themselves skills while bringing home the necessary pennies for the family coffers.

Today, we can hardly imagine the cold, discomfort and lack of food in war-torn Britain. We take hot water, electricity, mass communication, TV, cars, plentiful goods and choices for granted. But life in a gas lit, unheated, bombed-out world was tough, and the characters in this book leaned heavily on family values, community, friendship and worship to gain their courage and sense of self.

It has been an utter privilege to meet these men and women, and hear their stories. They are wonderful people, filled with dignity and memories about life in a world of manufacture, true grit and family pride. It has been an amazing experience to gather their stories and hear how they made their way in a rapidly changing world.

Despite hardship, suffering, challenge, they remain positive, outward looking and delightful individuals to this very day.

Further Reading

An Autobiography, Eva Grauberg (self-published)

Brothers At War, Robin Brackenbury (Ashbracken, 1992)

The City of Lace, David Lowe & Jack Richards (Nottingham Lace Centre Ltd, 1982)

Don't Be Late On Monday, Mark Ashfield (Breedon Books, 2004)

Framework Knitting, Marilyn Palmer (Shire Publications Ltd, 2002)

History of Nottingham Castle, Bernard Gott (G&B Offset Supplies, 1978)

The Illustrated History of Nottingham's Suburbs, Geoffrey Oldfield (Breedon Books, 2003)

Independent Street, Joan Wallace (Gowan Publishing Ltd, 1984)

Invisible Workers, Barbara Bagilhole (Benefits Research Unit, University of Nottingham, 1986)

Lost Buildings of Nottingham, Douglas Whitworth (The History Press, 2010)

The Nottinghamshire Domesday: A Reader's Guide, Graham Back & David Roffe (City of Nottingham Arts Department, 1986)

Nottingham's Heritage: A View of Conservation in the City, Nottingham City Planning Department (Nottingham City Planning Department, 1985)

Nottingham Lace, Zillah Halls (Nottingham Services Committee, 1985)

Nottingham and South Notts on Old Postcards, Grenville Jennings (Reflections of a Bygone Age, 1984)

Nottingham: The Way We Were, Andrew Gill (CreateSpace, 2015)

Ragtime Joe, Joan Wallace (Gowan Publishing Ltd, 1998)

A Rough Lot: The Story of the Young Women and Girls Who Worked in the Nottingham Lace Finishing Industry, Alan Brown (Sheila Brown, 2001)

St Ann's Nottingham: Inner-City Voice, Ruth I. Jones (Plowright Press, 2002)

Saturday Night and Sunday Morning, Alan Sillitoe (Pan Books Ltd, 1958)

The Sugar Girls, Duncan Barrett & Nuala Calvi (Harper, 2012)

Acknowledgements

With enormous thanks to Hannah MacDonald of September for your inspiration and patience, understanding and guidance with this book; to Jane Graham Maw of Graham Maw Christie for clear-sighted representation as ever.

Huge thanks to the 'stars' of the book, Derek Happs, Betty Allsop, Albert Godfrey, Pauline Braker, Doreen Rushton and Bob Cox, for opening your homes, your memories and your hearts, and for all the extra advice and help with the book. Thanks, too, to Daisy Godfrey and Philip Rushton for your great contributions and to Steve and Pauline Sewell for all your help. Heartfelt thanks to Joan Wallace and Alan Jennings for all your wonderful stories, research, writing, enthusiasm and support.

Thanks to Nottingham Library, the Museum of Nottingham Life, Natalie Braber of Trent University, Simon Brown of Nottingham Castle, for your research help. Huge thanks to Jess Gallagher for your research help kicking things off so well, to Katie Smith for your sterling efforts and research and to Olamiju Fajemesin for your research, administrative support and comments.

Thanks also to Stephen Engelhard of Angel Productions for your encouragement and your excellent Central TV film on Nottingham workers, *City of Women* (1987). Also, thanks to Andrea Stokes for lending me your book on lace making. Thanks too to G.H. Hurt and daughter for showing me your wonderful working looms.

Many thanks to Albert and Corinne Haynes for hospitality, patience, laughter, research support and office space, especially in the early stages of the book.

Thanks as always to others who played their particular part in keeping me going: Vicky Abram, Tim Davis of Acuherblondon.com, Gill Doust and all at Spectrum. Warmest thanks to Johnnie McKeown for your constructive patience and encouragement.

And finally, enormous hugs and kisses to Clara Potter-Sweet for bearing with, as well as your excellent editorial feedback. Plus purrs to the Keedees, Mackerel and Capuccino, for your endless night cat company.

About the Author

Corinne Sweet is a broadcaster, screenwriter, psychologist and psychotherapist and author of over fourteen books. These include popular psychology books, such as *Change Your Life with CBT*, *The Mindfulness Journal* and *The Anxiety Journal*, and the bestselling memoirs she has ghosted, *Sixty Years a Nurse* and *Deliver Me from Evil*. She is the Chair of the Book Committee of the Writers' Guild and her books have been translated into over twenty languages.

www.corinnesweet.com